Harry Thurston Peck

Examination papers

Used during the years 1877-1882 in Harvard, Yale, Columbia, Cornell,

Amherst and Williams colleges

Harry Thurston Peck

Examination papers
Used during the years 1877-1882 in Harvard, Yale, Columbia, Cornell, Amherst and Williams colleges

ISBN/EAN: 9783337121594

Printed in Europe, USA, Canada, Australia, Japan

Cover: Foto ©ninafisch / pixelio.de

More available books at **www.hansebooks.com**

EXAMINATION

PAPERS

USED DURING THE YEARS

1877-1882

IN

HARVARD, YALE, COLUMBIA, CORNELL, AMHERST AND WILLIAMS COLLEGES.

COMPILED AND ARRANGED

BY

HARRY THURSTON PECK, M.A.,

FELLOW OF COLUMBIA COLLEGE.

NEW YORK:
GILLISS BROTHERS,
75 & 77 FULTON STREET.

1882.

PREFACE.

During an experience of several years in preparing students for collegiate examinations, I have found nothing more serviceable in giving a finish and completeness to their preparation, than the use of papers employed in the examinations of previous years. Students have often remarked to me that nothing else afforded them so clear an idea of what was likely to be required of them ; for while the questions are not alike each year, their general scope and tenor are the same ; and there is a general similarity throughout them all.

I have been led to think, therefore, that what I have myself found useful may be of some slight service to others ; and it is in this belief that the papers here collected are now published. Complete sets of entrance questions used at Harvard, Yale, Columbia, Cornell, Amherst, and Williams Colleges ; sets of papers used at the intermediate and concluding examinations of the freshman, sophomore, junior and senior classes in Columbia College ; and the questions asked in the scholarship and other prize examinations at Columbia, have been included in this little volume, so that the student who is preparing to pass examinations, and the instructor who is assisting him, may engage in their work with a better understanding of what is to be required of them both.

The colleges enumerated above have been chosen for the reason that of all American universities, these are acknowledged to stand highest, both in their requirements for admission and in the scholarship and literary attainments of their graduates. Whoever can successfully pass the examinations at these institutions need not fear to present himself before the faculty of any other in this country.

It will be noticed that among the Columbia sets, those in mathematics are the most numerous. The reason of this will be sufficiently obvious to the Columbia student who remembers that it is in mathematics that more undergraduates are conditioned than in any other study of the curriculum. Still another reason is found in the fact that copies of these papers are seldom seen, it not being permitted to take them from the room.

In conclusion, I desire to express my thanks to members of the different faculties for many favors courteously extended ; and to express the hope that the study of the papers herein contained will be of service alike to undergraduates and to those whose special work lies in the line of collegiate preparation.

H. T. P.

COLUMBIA COLLEGE, Sept. 1, 1882.

HARVARD.

[The University now furnishes copies of entrance papers to any one upon application. The requirements for admission include many options under the new elective system. To those who do not seek an advanced standing at entrance, but only desire to enter without honors, the following requirements are recommended, and will be found the easiest preparatory course possible : *Latin*, Cæsar's Gallic War, IV Books ; Æneid, VI Books; Grammar, Prosody, Easy Translation at Sight, Prose Composition. *Greek*, Easy Greek at Sight (from the Anabasis), Easy Prose Composition, Iliad I–III. Ancient History (Greece and Rome). *Mathematics*, Arithmetic entire, except the technical parts of commercial arithmetic ; Algebra, through Quadratics ; Geometry, thirteen chapters of Pierce's Geometry. *Physics*, Rolfe and Gillette's Nat. Philos. *English Composition*, a composition written in the room upon a subject given out at the time of examination. To secure admission, forty-five per cent. of the questions must be correctly answered.]

ENTRANCE EXAMINATION.

(1882.)

LATIN.

I. Translate Cæsar, Bk. III., 3.

Write out the words *quo in consilio* . . . *possent*, marking quantity of every vowel. Explain syntax of *nihil, subsidio, veniri, pervenissent.* Give future indicative of *timendum, exquirere, relictis, posset, placuit, experiri.* Give *nom.* and *gen. sing.* and *gender* of *obsidibus, loca, subsidio, salute, eventum.* Who was Galba? What were the circumstances here mentioned and what the result?

II. Translate *Æneid*, Bk. IV., 416-424.

Explain circumstances under which these words were said. Give metrical scheme of lines 420, 421, 422, 423. Mark caesura in line 417.

III. Translate *Æneid*, Bk. VI., 863-874.

Describe briefly the circumstances here alluded to. Write metrical scheme of lines 870 and 871. How does the scanning help settle the syntax in line 874?

(LATIN AT SIGHT.)

IV. Translate :—

Itaque illorum responsis tum et ludi per dies decem facti sunt neque res ulla quae ad placandos deos pertineret praetermissa est. eidemque iusserunt simulacrum Iovis facere maius et in excelso collocare et contra atque antea fuerat ad orientem convertere: ac se sperare dixerunt, si illud signum, quod videtis, solis ortum et forum curiamque conspiceret, fore ut ea consilia quae clam essent inita contra salutem urbis atque imperii, illustrarentur, ut a senatu populoque Romano perspici possent. Atque illud signum collocandum consules illi locaverunt, sed tanta fuit operis tarditas, ut neque superioribus consulibus neque nobis ante hodiernum diem collocaretur.

Explain mood and tense of *pertineret, conspiceret, fore, essent inita, illustrarentur, possent.* Explain construction of *collocandum.* Explain meaning here of *responsis, ludi.* Show position of statue from description here given. Give general idea of this passage.

V. *Cicero.*

Translate :—

Tu, tu, inquam, M. Antoni, princeps C. Caesari omnia perturbare cupienti causam belli contra patriam inferendi dedisti. Quid enim aliud ille dicebat? Quam causam sui dementissimi consili et facti adferebat, nisi quod intercessio neglecta, ius tribunicium sublatum, circumscriptus[1] a senatu esset Antonius? Omitto quam haec falsa, quam levia, praesertim cum omnino nulla causa iusta cuiquam esse possit contra patriam arma capiendi. Sed nihil de Caesare: tibi certe confitendum est causam perniciosissimi belli in persona tua constitesse O miserum te, si haec intelligis, miseriorem, si non intelligis hoc litteris mandari, hoc memoriae prodi, huius rei ne posteritatem quidem omnium saeculorum umquam immemorem fore, consules ex Italia expulsos, cumque iis Cn. Pompeium, quod imperii populi Romani decus ac lumen fuit, omnes consulares, qui per valetudinem[2] exsequi cladem illam fugamque potuissent, praetores, praetorios, tribunos plebis, magnam partem senatus, omnem subolem inventutis, unoque verbo rem publicam expulsam atque exterminatam suis sedibus !

---

[1] circumscribo, *hamper one's actions.*
[2] valetudo, *state of health.*

Explain construction of *inferendi* and compare with it that of *capiendi* below. Explain mood and tense of *potuissent, circumscriptos esset, possit. Cuiquam,* why not *alicui* or *cuique?* Give derivation of *princeps, tribunicium, iusta, posteritatem,* showing force of suffix or suffixes in each case.

VI. *Virgil.* Translate Æneid, Bk. IX., 644–652.

Scan last *seven* lines, and point out at least two peculiarities of versification.

VII. *Ovid.* Translate Metamorphoses, Bk. XIII., 1–12.

VIII. Translate into Latin.

(a) Have you forgotten who commanded the Carthagenians at Zama? Having got possession of the town, he ordered the prefect to close all the gates. He advised the counsel to go to Ephesus, the chief town of that region. The soldier confessed that he was sorry for his cowardice, and begged Cæsar to pardon him.

(b). The matter was laid before the senate, and it was decided that ambassadors should be sent. But men could not be found to send, since every one refused the duty from fear. For Pompey, on departing from the city, had said in the senate that he would equally regard as enemies those who had remained at Rome and those who had been in Cæsar's camp. Thus three days were spent in discussion and inactivity. Even Lucius Metellus, tribune of the people, was persuaded by the enemies of Cæsar to resist the decree of the senate and hinder whatever Cæsar wished to do. When Cæsar found out his design, having wasted several days in vain, he departed from the city, leaving unfinished what he had intended to do, and in order to lose no more time hastened to Massilia in farther Gaul.

IX. Translate into English, *Nepos*, Pelop. XVI., 5.

[NOTE: Questions IV., V., VI., VII., and VIII (b), are not *prescribed;* but the student seeking admission will find these options less difficult than any other.]

GREEK.

(EASY GREEK AT SIGHT.)

I. *Translate* into English :—

☞ You are advised not to write any part of the translation until you have read the passage through two or three times.

[SUBJECT.—A council of war between Cyrus and Cyaxares.]

TRANSLATE :—

Κῦρος δὲ καὶ Κυαξάρης συνταξάμενοι περιέμενον, ὡς, εἰ προσίοιεν οἱ πολέμιοι, μαχούμενοι. ὡς δὲ δῆλον ἐγένετο ὅτι οὐκ ἐξίοιεν οἱ πολέμιοι ἐκ τοῦ ἐρύματος[1] οὐδὲ μάχην ποιήσοιντο ἐν ταύτῃ τῇ ἡμέρᾳ, ὁ μὲν Κυαξάρης καλέσας τὸν Κῦρον καὶ τῶν ἄλλων τοὺς ἐπικαιρίους[2] ἔλεξε τοιάδε· Δοκεῖ μοι, ἔφη, ὦ ἄνδρες, ὥσπερ τυγχάνομεν συντεταγμένοι οὕτως ἰέναι πρὸς τὸ ἔρυμα τῶν ἀνδρῶν καὶ δηλοῦν ὅτι θέλομεν μάχεσθαι. οὕτω γάρ, ἔφη, ἐὰν μὴ ἀντεπεξίωσιν ἐκεῖνοι, οἱ μὲν ἡμέτεροι μᾶλλον θαρρήσαντες[3] ἀπίασιν, οἱ πο-

λέμιοι δὲ τὴν τόλμαν ἰδόντες ἡμῶν μᾶλλον φοβήσονται. τούτῳ
μὲν οὕτος ἐδόκει. ὁ δὲ Κῦρος, Μηδαμῶς, ἔφη, πρὸς τῶν θεῶν, ὦ
Κυαξάρη, οὕτω ποιήσωμεν. εἰ γὰρ ἤδη ἐκφανέντες πορευσόμεθα,
ὡς σὺ κελεύεις, νῦν τε⁴ προσιόντας ἡμᾶς οἱ πολέμιοι θεάσονται
οὐδὲν φοβούμενοι, εἰδότες ὅτι ἐν ἀσφαλεῖ εἰσι τοῦ μεδὲν παθεῖν·
ἐπειδάν τε⁴ μεδὲν ποιήσαντες ἀπίωμεν, πάλιν καθορῶντες ἐμῶν τὸ
πλῆθος πολὺ ἐυδεέςτερον τοῦ ἑαυτῶν καταφρονήσουσι. καὶ⁴ αὔριον
ἐξίασι πολὺ ἐρρωμενεστέραις⁵ ταῖς γνώμαις.

¹ *intrenchment.*　² *important* (ἐπί, καιρός).　³ θάρρος, *courage.*　⁴ τὲ ...
τὲ ... καί, *both* ... *and* ... *and.*　⁵ ρώννυμι, *strengthen.*

II. Translate, Iliad I., 266–274.

Who is the speaker of these lines?

Where are τράφεν (266), ξίνιεν (273), πείθοντο (273) made, and from
what present indicatives?

Account for case of Βουλέων (273).

III. Translate Il. II., 455–466.

Composition or derivation of ἄσπετον (455) and δουλιχοδείρων (460).

Account for case of ὀυρανόν (458).

Account for accent of ἄπο (464).

What river near Troy besides the Scamander does Homer frequently
mention?

IV. Translate Il. III., 351–360.

Copy verse 351 ; divide it into feet; mark the quantity of every
syllable ; and indicate caesura.

Explain mood of ἐρρίγησι (353) and παράσχῃ (354).

Composition of ἀμπεπαλών (355) : where is it made and from what
present indicative?

V. Translate Herodotus IV., 131, 132.

[SUBJECT.—The Scythians send to King Darius five arrows, a bird, a frog, and
a mouse. The Persians are at a loss as to the meaning of these gifts.]

VI. Translate into Greek :—

(a). They asked him who did this.

He is willing to wait until I send to the king.

They took-care¹ that they should themselves be free.²

If you have done none of these things, what do you fear?

All the citizens remained five days.

The Thirty ordered³ them to lead⁴ Leon away,⁴ that he might be-
executed.⁵

They took Orontes by the girdle.[6]
I shall have had everything which I wished.

[1] ἐπιμελέομαι. [2] ἐλεύθερος. [3] προστάσσω. [4] ἀπάγω. [5] ἀποθνῄσκω (aor.). [6] ζώνη.

(b). Tissaphernes happened to be in Sardis[1] when the battle occurred. So that the Persians said that they had been betrayed[2] by him, and the king himself having sent Tithraustes cuts off the head of Tissaphernes. After this Tithraustes sends ambassadors to Agesilaos, saying : " The king thinks it right[3] that you yourself return home, but that the cities in Asia, being independent,[4] pay him the old tribute."[5] Agesilaos answered that he would not do this without authority[6] from Sparta.[7]

[1] Σάρδεις. [2] προδίδωμι. [3] ἀξιόω. [4] αὐτόνομος. [5] δασμός. [6] τὰ τέλη. [7] οἴκοι.

[NOTE : Questions V, and VI (b) are not prescribed, but have been selected as the least difficult of the options.]

ANCIENT HISTORY AND GEOGRAPHY.

[*Omit one question from each of the following groups.*]

I.

1. What are the principal divisions of Asia Minor? Name and locate five of the chief cities of Italy.

2. Draw a map showing military roads in Italy and principal towns through which they pass.

II.

1. Who are the chief authorities for the history of the regal period and when did they write? What were their sources of information? What other sources of information have we?

2. Tell what you know about Gajus Marius.

3. Give an account of the reign of Hadrian (A. D. 117–138.)

III.

1. What forms of Government were represented in Greece? Give the leading features of each.

2. State briefly political results of following battles : Marathon ; Aegos-potami ; Mantineia ; Chaeroneia ; Pydna. Give dates of battles.

3. Aristides ; Lysander ; Pelopidas ; Brasidas. Give brief account of two.

PHYSICS.

1. Show the experiment of the Magdeburg hemispheres and tell what the experiment shows.

2. How far would a body fall in three seconds in a vacuum?

3. Explain "beats" produced by musical sounds.

4. Upon what does the color of bodies depend?

5. What is the apparent position of a point seen by reflection in a plane mirror? Show how to determine the apparent position of an arrow under the same circumstances.

6. Are liquids and gases good or bad conductors of heat? What is convection of heat?

7. Describe the construction and use of the gold-leaf electroscope.

GEOMETRY.

1. What must you know about the sides or angles of two triangles in order to be able to infer that they are equal?

Prove that two triangles are equal when the three sides of the one are respectively equal to the three sides of the other.

2. Two chords of a circle which intersect within the circumference divide the latter into four parts whose lengths taken in order are 89°, 43°, 117°, and 111°. Find, without proof, the angles which chords make with each other.

Prove that an angle formed by two secants intersecting without the circumference, is measured by one-half the difference of the intercepted arcs.

3. Define similar polygons and prove that two triangles are similar when they are mutually equiangular.

4. State, without proof, how you would inscribe a regular decagon in a given circle.

5. *Prove* that in a right-angled triangle the straight line joining the right angle to the centre of the square on the hypothenuse will bisect the right angle.

ARITHMETIC.

1. Simplify $\dfrac{4\frac{2}{11}}{5\frac{7}{8}+\dfrac{3\frac{1}{2}}{2\frac{2}{3}}}$

2. It takes 54 yards 2½ feet of carpet to cover a floor 23½ feet long and 15¾ feet wide. Find the width of the carpet.

3. If a pound equals 0.4536 kilogrammes, how many grains are there in 3⅔ grammes?

[1 lb.= 7000 grains.]

4. Find the greatest common divisor of 323 and 437.

5. I gained 33⅓ per cent. in selling a horse, and with the proceeds

bought another horse which I afterwards sold for $120, thereby losing 25 per cent. Did I gain or lose by the transactions?

ALGEBRA.

1. Simplify

$$\frac{a^2 - bc}{(a-b)(a-c)} + \frac{b^2 + ca}{(b+c)(b-a)} + \frac{c^2 + ab}{(c-a)(c+b)}$$

2. A man bought a certain number of sheep for $300; he kept 15 sheep, and sold the remainder for $270, gaining half a dollar a head. How many sheep did he buy and at what price?

3. Find greatest common divisor of

$$2x^5 - 11x^2 - 9 \text{ and } 4x^5 + 11x^4 + 81.$$

4. Solve the equation

$$\frac{(4a^2 - b^2)(x^2 + 1)}{4a^2 + b^2} = 2x$$

Reduce answers to their lowest terms.

5. Find square root of

$$x^3 + 2x^{\frac{5}{2}} - 3x^2 - 4x^{\frac{3}{2}} + 4x.$$

6. A and B can do a piece of work in 18 days; A and C can do it in 45 days; B and C in 20 days. Find the time in which A, B, and C can do it, working together.

ENGLISH COMPOSITION.

I.

Write a short composition on one of the subjects given below :—

(a). Othello's Defence before the Senate.
(b). Comparison of Desdemona with Emilia.
(c). Character of Iago.
(d). Iago's Plot.
(e). Character of Cassio.
(f). Parallel between Othello and Falconbridge.
(g). The Death of Othello.

II.

Correct any errors you discover in any *twelve* of the following sentences :—

(a). The vote of the trustees on the resolution sustaining President Bartlett, was 6 in the affirmative, 4 in the negative, with one member of the board absent, whom it is claimed by the opposition would have voted in the negative.

(b). " I only said I wouldn't go, without one of the servants come up to Sir Leicester Dedlock," returns Mr. Smallweed.

(*c*). Neither Senators Dawes nor Hoar were in their seats to-day.

(*d*). She was smaller in stature than either of her three sisters, to all of whom had been acceded the praise of being fine women.

(*e*). Happily, neither she nor her mother had completely parted with their senses.

(*f*). If I review Virgil, for instance, in April, I will forget much of it before July, having so much other work on my hands.

(*g*). "Lying off the Battery, we would be as easily accessible as vessels at the city piers."

"When will you be ready for business?" asked the reporter. " By the spring of 1883; not before. * * * We shall have a stock company, but there will be comparatively little stock issued. We shall place a large amount of bonds. This will enable us to avoid onerous taxation from the city."

(*h*). He folded it and put it in his breast pocket and laid down once more, and it was not referred to again.

(*i*). Although Mr. Jonas conducted Charity to the hotel and sat himself beside her at the board, it was pretty clear that he had an eye to "the other one " also, for he often glanced across at Mercy and seemed to draw comparisons between the personal appearance of the two, which were not unfavorable to the superior plumpness of the younger sister.

(*k*). " This is a phenomena common to an immense number of diseases."

(*l*). "Mr. Stanley was the only one of his predecessors who slaughtered the natives of the region he passed through.

(*m*.) "She was a good deal hurt, and her hand so severely injured that unless she has the forefinger amputated she will entirely lose the use of it."

(*n*). " The farmstead was always the wooden, white painted house of which all the small country towns are composed.

(*o*). If I were old enough to be married, I am old enough to manage my husband's house.

(*p*). The seventeenth century evidently had a different notion of books and women than that which flourishes in the nineteenth.

(*q*). "It would not suit the rules of art nor of my own feelings to write in that style."

FRENCH.

[A good translation of No. 1 is all that is necessary to pass. 2 and 3 are set to enable candidates to make up for some deficiencies in translation. Write 4 if you can.]

1. TRANSLATE :—

Le docteur sauta en bas ; et prenant sous son bras son livre, et à la main ses pistolets, it s'en vint tout seul à la porte de la cabane. A peine il y eut frappé, qu'un homme à la physionomie fort douce vint lui ouvrir la porte, et s'éloigna de lui aussitôt, en lui disant : "Seigneur, je ne suis qu'un pauvre paria, qui ne suis pas digne de vous recevoir : mais si vous jugez à propos de vous mettre à l'abri chez moi, vous m'honorerez beaucoup.—Mon frère, lui répondit l'Anglais, j'accepte de bon cœur." Cependant le paria sortit avec une torche à la main, une charge de bois sec sur son dos, et un panier plein sous son bras ; il s'approcha des gens de la suite du docteur, qui étaient à quelque distance de là sous un arbre, et leur dit : "Puisque vous ne voulez pas me faire l'honneur d'entrer chez moi, voilà des fruits enveloppés de leurs écorces que vous pouvez manger sans être souillés, et voilà du feu pour vous sécher et vous préserver des tigres. Que Dieu vous conserve !" Il rentra aussitôt dans sa cabane, et dit au docteur : "Je vous le répète, je ne suis qu'un malheureux : mais omme à votre teint blanc et à vos habits je vois que vous n'êtes pas Indien, j'espère que vous n'aurez pas de répugnance pour les aliments que vous présentera votre pauvre serviteur." En même temps il mit à terre, sur une natte, des pommes, des patates cuites sous la cendre, des bananes grillées, et un pot de riz ; après quoi il se retira sur sa natte, auprès de sa femme et de son enfant, endormi près d'elle dans un berceau. "Homme vertueux, lui dit l'Anglais, vous valez beaucoup mieux que moi, puisque vous faites du bien à ceux qui vous méprisent. Si vous ne m'honorez pas de votre présence sur cette même natte, je croirai que vous me prenez moi-même pour un homme méchant, et je sors à l'instant de votre cabane, dussé-je être noyé par la pluie, ou dévoré par les tigres."

2. Principal tenses of all verbs in first 4 lines (thus INF. *être* ; PRES. PART. *étant* ; PAST PART. *été* ; IND. PRES. *je suis* ; PRET. *je fus*).

3. Principal rules for formation of feminine of adjectives.

4. Write 8 or 10 lines in French about President Garfield.

YALE.

[REQUIREMENTS FOR ADMISSION : *Greek*, Grammar and Prosody, Prose Composition; Xenophon, Bks. I.-IV. of Anabasis; Iliad, Bks. I.-III.; Easy Greek at Sight, Greek History. *Latin*, Grammar and Prosody, Four Bks. of Cæsar's Gallic War, or Sallust's Jugurtha, Seven Orations of Cicero, Bucolics and Six Bks. of Æneid, Metamorphoses of Ovid, 2500 lines, Easy Latin at Sight, Prose Composition, Roman History. *Mathematics*, Higher Arithmetic complete, Algebra (Loomis's to Logarithms), Euclid, Bks. I. and II. English and Modern Geography are no longer required. To secure admission candidates must successfully answer fifty per cent. of all the questions.]

1881.

LATIN.

(*Grammar.*)

[In writing Latin words, mark quantity of penult in forms of more than two syllables.]

1. Give genitive singular of *miles, fides, senex, bos, rus.*

2. Decline in full : *caput, plus, tristis.*

3. Give nominative, genitive and dative singular, in full, of each of the demonstrative pronouns.

4. Tell exactly where each of the following forms is made, and from what present it comes : *velitis, potuere, euntes, scriberemur, nosse.*

5. Give synopsis of second person singular subjunctive active of a verb of each of the four regular conjugations.

6. Principal parts of *tango, sumo, sentio, vinco.*

7. Explain use of modes in conditional sentences.

8. State what you can concerning form and use of the locative case.

[Omit any two of the passages.]

1. Translate Cæsar, B. G., I., 34.
Change the words of Ariovistus to direct discourse.

2. Translate Cæsar, B. G., IV., 23.

Why is *convenient* in the subjunctive ?

Describe the *vigiliæ* and *horæ.* Give approximate English equivalent of *hora nona.*

3. Translate Sallust J., 35.

Sketch concisely the career of Jugurtha.

4. Translate Sallust J., 95.

[One of the following passages may be omitted.]

5. Translate Cic. in Cat. III., 10.

Give the principal verbs of this sentence : Upon what does *quantum* —*potuisset* depend? What explains the meaning of *lex haec?* Explain the subjunctives *possent, putassent.* Why did Cicero go into exile? How long was this after his consulship?

6. Pro Marcell. I.

With what does *idem* agree? Construction of the antecedent of *quæ.* Why the pluperfect tense in *eram usus?* What moved Cicero to deliver this oration? What was the fate of Marcellus?

7. Pro Arch. III.

Explain fully the meaning of the sentence *Nactus est—posset.* Why is the subjunctive required? Why *alter* and not *alius?*

8. Pro Lig. XII.

What determines the gender of *nulla?* With what does *melius* agree? Why are the two negatives *nulla—nec* not equivalent to an affirmative?

(*Virgil.*)

1. Translate Æneid II., 491–499.

Who is referred to by *patria?* Give construction of *ariete* and of *cumulo.* Describe the *aries.*

Divide first three lines into feet, and give rules for quantities of all vowels in the first line.

[Omit any two of the following.]

2. Translate Eclogue IV., 26–33.

Why are these poems sometimes called " Bucolics ?" Why " Eclogues ?"

3. Translate Georg. II., 136–144.

What is the allusion in *tauri spirantes ignem?*

4. Translate Æn. IX., 226–233.

Give in brief the episode of Nisus and Euryalus.

5. Translate Ovid, Met. II., 319–328.

Give the story of Phaëthon. When and where did Ovid die?

(LATIN AT SIGHT.)

M. Atilius Regulus, cum consul iterum in Africa ex insidiis captus esset, duce Xanthippo Lacedæmonio, imperatore autem patre Hannibalis Hamilcare, juratus missus est ad senatum, ut, nisi redditi essent Pœnis

captivi nobiles quidam, rediret ipse Karthaginem.   Is cum Roman venis-
set, utilitatis speciem videbat, sed eam, ut res declarat, falsam judicavit:
quæ erat talis : manere in patria, esse domi suæ cum uxore, cum liberis ;
quam calamitatem accepisset in bello, communem fortunæ bellicæ judi-
cantem, tenere consularis dignitatis gradum.   Itaque quid fecit ? In senatum venit, mandata exposuit : sententiam ne diceret, recusavit ; " quam
diu jure jurando hostium teneretur, non esse se senatorem."

(LATIN COMPOSITION.)

While Xenophon was making a sacrifice he learned that the elder of
his two sons, Gryllus by name, had fallen in battle.   He then inquired
how he had died.   When he was told that he fell while fighting most
bravely, he declared that he felt greater joy at the bravery of his son
than grief at his death.

(ROMAN HISTORY.)

1. Give an account of Rome's wars with Pyrrhus.

2. What was Rome's first province, and how did it come into her
possession ?

3. Sketch the career of Tiberius Gracchus.

4. By what means did Augustus become Emperor?

GREEK.

(GREEK GRAMMAR.)

[All Greek words to be written with accents.]

1. Decline throughout τιμή, δῶρον, γένος, the pronoun σύ, and the nu-
meral εἷς.

2. Give the synopsis (*i. e.* first form in every mode) of the 1st aor. act.
of στέλλω, the 2d aor. mid. of τίθημι.

3. Analyze λυθείησαν.

4. What sort of pronouns are οἷος and ὅσος ?   Give the demonstrative and interrogative pronouns corresponding.

5. What is *hiatus*, and what means are used in Greek to avoid it ?

6. Give some rules, with examples, of euphonic change in consonants.
What consonants may end a Greek word ?

7. Give a list of prepositions that take one case only.

8. Explain, with Greek examples, the terms *enclitic, cognate accusa-
tive, objective genitive, supplementary participle.*

9. With what parts of the verb is the particle ἄν not used ?

(GREEK COMPOSITION.)

[All Greek words to be written with accents.]

1. Cyrus with his army was besieging this city.   And of the citizens

some wished to surrender(¹) it,˙but others spoke against(²) it. Cyrus therefore said that when he had taken the city, he should do well by(³) those who spoke against surrender and exile(⁴) the others.

(¹) παραδίδωμι.   (²) ἀντιλέγω.
(³) εὖ ποιεῖν.
(⁴) ἐκβάλλω.

2. If the general had wished to go, the soldiers would have followed (him).

3. Let us march as quickly as possible to the river that we may embark upon the boats which Cyrus has given us.

ANABASIS.

1. Translate Xen. Anab. I., 4.,8.

What distinction does Xen. here make between ἀποδιδράσκω and ἀποφεύγω? Why does he use μά and not νή before τοὺς θεοὺς? Rule for mode in παρῃ? Where is ἰόντων found, and from what verb? For what longer form does κακίους stand? At what point in the march did this desertion take place?

2. Translate Xen. Anab. II., 3.,10.

Why is there an article with δόρυ and none with βακτηρίαν? Explain mode in δοκοίη, and mode and tense in ἔπαισεν ἄν. What sort of pronoun is αὐτός as here used? Tell what is known of life and death of Klearchos.

3. Translate Xen. Anab. III., 5.,7.

What was the ordinary length of the Greek spear? Construction of τοῦ βάθους, of μισθόν, of ὅτου? For what longer form does ὅτου stand? Explain the mode in δέοιτο. How may the gender of ἅ be accounted for?

4. Translate Xen. Anab. IV., 6.,17.

Explain the mode in δειπνήσωμεν. Present and perfect of καταλεψόμενος? Relation of τούτων, of ἡμῖν? How did Xenophon come to be in command? Who else was associated with him?

[This may be substituted for 3 and 4 above.]

5. Translate Hdt. VI., 104.

Make a list of the Ionic forms in this passage, adding in each case the Attic form,with accents. Where was Imbros? Construction of ἑαυτοῦ, of τυραννίδος.

HOMER'S ILIAD.

1. Translate Iliad I., 292–303.

Make a list of all the Homeric forms in this passage, giving in each case the corresponding Attic word with accents. Where is πέρυησαι found, and what in the form itself shows it? Give the presents of ἐπείξομαι, πείσεσθαι, ἀφέλεσθε.

2. Translate Iliad II., 188-197.

Write out a metrical scheme of the sixth line, accounting for the quantity of each syllable. Point out the metrical peculiarity in the ninth line. Give the Attic form of ἐπέεσσιν. Explain the accent on ὥς.

3. Translate Iliad III., 146-153.

Point out the irregularity of syntax in the third line. Give the Attic form for τεττίγεσσιν. What is the first foot of the seventh line? What two forms of the same word in this passage?

GREEK AT SIGHT.

[Hermogenes explains who his friends are of whom he is proud.]

ἐκ τούτου εἶπέ τις· "σὸν ἔργον, ὦ Ἑρμόγενες, λέγειν τε τοὺς φίλους οἵτινές εἰσι καὶ ἐπιδεικνύναι ὡς μέγα τε δύνανται καὶ σοῦ ἐπιμέλονται, ἵνα δοκῇς δικαίως ἐπ᾿ αὐτοῖς μέγα φρονεῖν." "Οὐκοῦν ὡς μὲν καὶ Ἕλληνες καὶ βάρβαροι τοὺς θεοὺς ἡγοῦνται πάντα εἰδέναι τά τε ὄντα καὶ τὰ μέλλοντα εὔδηλον.(¹) πᾶσαι γοῦν αἱ πόλεις καὶ πάντα τὰ ἔθνη διὰ μαντικῆς ἐπερωτῶσι τοὺς θεοὺς τί τε χρὴ καὶ τί οὐ χρὴ ποιεῖν. καὶ μὴν ὅτι νομίζομέν γε δύνασθαι αὐτοὺς καὶ εὖ καὶ κακῶς ποιεῖν καὶ τοῦτο σαφές.(¹) πάντες γοῦν αἰτοῦνται τοὺς θεοὺς τὰ μὲν φαῦλα ἀποτρέπειν τἀγαθὰ δὲ διδόναι. οὗτοι τοίνυν οἱ πάντα μὲν εἰδότες πάντα δὲ δυνάμενοι θεοὶ οὕτω μοι φίλοι εἰσὶν ὥστε διὰ τὸ ἐπιμελεῖσθαί μου οὔποτε λήθω(²) αὐτοὺς οὔτε νυκτὸς οὐδ᾿ ἡμέρας οὐδ᾿ ὅποι ἂν ὁρμῶμαι οὐδ᾿ ὅτι ἂν μέλλω πράττειν. διὰ δὲ τὸ προειδέναι καὶ ὅ τι ἐξ ἑκάστου ἀποβήσεται σημαίνουσί μοι πέμποντες ἀγγέλους φήμας καὶ ἐνύπνια(³) καὶ οἰωνοὺς ἅ τε δεῖ καὶ ἃ οὐ χρὴ ποιεῖν, οἷς ἐγὼ ὅταν μὲν πείθωμαι, οὐδέποτέ μοι μεταμέλει· ἤδη δέ ποτε καὶ ἀπιστήσας ἐκολάσθην."(⁴)

(¹) Sc. ἐστί. (²) =λανθάνω. (³) dreams. (⁴) I have been punished.

(GREEK HISTORY.)

1. Give a brief account of Aristeides, and of Brasidas.

2. What is meant by the period of tyrants in Greek History? Describe the rise and overthrow of some one of them.

3. Describe the formation of the first Athenian confederacy and the process of its change into an empire.

4. Mention principal battles (with dates) of Alexander's invasion of Asia. What motive did he claim to have for his attack on the Persian king? What were results of his career?

ALGEBRA.

1. Free from negative exponents the expression $(4a^{-3}b^2x^{-4})^{-4}$.

2. Reduce to its lowest terms the fraction $\dfrac{x^2-2x-15}{x^2+10x+21}$.

3. Factor n^3-2n^2+n, x^8-1, $x^3-n^3y^3$, and x^6+y^6.

4. Make the denominator rational of $\dfrac{2}{\sqrt{5}-\sqrt{2}}$.

5. Multiply $\sqrt{x}-2+\sqrt{-3}$ by $\sqrt{x}+2-\sqrt{-3}$.

6. Solve $\dfrac{5}{x}-\dfrac{3x+1}{x^2}=\dfrac{1}{4}$.

7. Solve $\begin{cases} x^2-xy=153 \\ x+y=1 \end{cases}$.

8. By the Binomial Theorem expand to four terms,
$$\frac{1}{\sqrt{n-x^2}}.$$

9. Sum the infinite series $1+\dfrac{1}{2}+\dfrac{1}{4}+$ etc.

EUCLID.

1. To describe a parallelogram that shall be equal to a given triangle, and have one of its angles equal to a given rectilineal angle.

2. If a straight line be bisected, and produced to any point, the square on the whole line thus produced and the square on the part of it produced, are together double of the square on half the line bisected and of the square on the line made up of the half and the part produced.

3. A given angle BAC is bisected; if CA is produced to G, and the angle BAG is bisected, prove that the two bisecting lines are at right angles.

ARITHMETIC.

1. Divide $\left(\dfrac{3}{4}\text{ of }\dfrac{5}{16}\text{ of }\dfrac{8}{2}\right)$ by $\dfrac{3\frac{3}{4}}{5\frac{7}{10}}$, and add the quotient to $\dfrac{3}{4}-\dfrac{7}{15}$.

2. Find $\sqrt{\dfrac{1}{21}}$, to three decimal places.

3. Find, to three decimal places, the number which has to 0.649 the same ratio which 58 has to 634.

4. A man bought a piece of ground containing 0.316 A, at 53 cents a square foot; what did he pay for the piece?

5. A grocer buys sugar at 18 cents a kilo, and sells it at 1 cent per 50 grams. How much per cent. does he gain?

CORNELL.

[REQUIREMENTS FOR ADMISSION : *English Grammar and Composition. Political and Physical Geography. Elementary Physiology* (exclusive of nervous system and names of bones and muscles). *Mathematics.* Charvenet's *Elementary* Geometry, Bks. I–V., Elementary Algebra, first twelve sections of Loomis, Arithmetic complete. *Greek.* One hundred pages of any Attic prose, Easy Greek at sight, Prose Composition, Iliad, Bks. I–III., and Greek History. *Latin*, Cæsar, Bks. I–IV., Eclogues and Æneid Bks. I–VI., Cicero, six orations, Easy Latin at sight, Prose Composition, Outlines of Roman History and Ancient Geography.]

1881.

ENGLISH.

1. Embody in a connected account the following particulars : (*a*) name in full, (*b*) birth-place, (*c*) age, (*d*) school or schools where fitted, (*e*) intended course of study, (*f*) purpose in seeking a college education.

2. Why is a verb inflected ?

3. Use *better*, in an example, as (*a*) a verb ; (*b*) an adjective ; (*c*) an adverb.

4. State the two principal uses of the compound personal pronouns.

5. In what respect does *which*, as an interrogative, differ from *who* and *what ?*

6. How can an adjective be turned into a descriptive clause ?

7. State when *shall*, and when *will*, is to be used as an auxiliary in the first person.

8. How are progressive forms in the present and preterite made ?

9. Mention the principal classes of subordinating conjunctions, and give an example of each class.

10. Distinguish between the same word used as an adverb and as a conjunction.

11. Write out a complex sentence, with a subordinate clause in the past tense, indicative mode, underlining the clause.

12. Explain the use of *few* and *a few ; elder* and *older ; latter* and *later ; a thousand men ; many a man.*

13. What kinds of nouns have no singular ?

14. Parse the following : *Which of these do you want ?*

15. Explain the meaning of the following terms: *impersonal, indirect object, genitive, gerund, complement, finite, orthoëpy, distributive, analysis, predicative, factitive, augmentative.*

16. Write out corrrectly the following sentences : (*a*) Never was a man so teased or suffered half so much uneasiness as I have done to-day. (*b*) How will we know who is the greatest of the two? (*c*) I, and not they, am to remain. (*d*) Either one of the four first in the class were good scholars. (*e*) I never have, nor never will attack him. (*f*) Scarcely was Elizabeth seated on the throne, than she began to feel the alarming embarrassments of her position. (*g*) Four months interest are due. (*h*) Nothing need be said so firmly, and nothing oftener than this.

17. State reasons for making any change in writing out preceding sentences.

18. Write out in prose the following verses, making complete grammatical sentences, supplying all ellipses, and changing inversions :

> " Heaven witness,
> I have been to you a true and humble wife,
> At all times to your will conformable :
> Ever in fear to kindle your dislike,
> Yea, subject to your countenance ; glad, or sorry,
> As I saw it inclined. When was the hour,
> I ever contradicted your desire,
> Or made it not mine too ? What friend of mine,
> That had to him derived your anger, did I
> Continue in my liking ? Nay, gave notice
> He was from thence discharged ?"

19. Analyze the following :
> " Wisely and slow : they stumble that run fast."

GEOGRAPHY.

1. Draw an outline map of North America.

2. Name the five grand divisions in the order of their size.

3. Between what parallels of latitude does Russia lie ? What are its climate, population, productions?

4. Bound Italy and name its capital.

5. State the positions of Algiers and Tunis, with the character and number of the population.

6. Name the three great rivers of South America.

7. Describe the great mountain system of the Western Continent.

8. Describe the Desert of Sahara.

9. Which is further north—New York or Paris? Washington or Madrid ? San Francisco or Hong Kong ?

10. What is meant by the tropics of Cancer and Capricorn ? The Arctic circle? The Antarctic circle ?

11. What is the Arctic current? How caused? What becomes of it?

12. What are the trade winds and how are they caused?

13. How could one sail by the shortest route from Rio Janeiro to St. Petersburg?

14. What States would a right line between Portland, Me., and Portland, Oregon, cross?

15. In coasting between Charleston, S. C., and the Columbia river, what countries would you pass on the right?

ELEMENTARY PHYSIOLOGY.

1. Give diagrams of the teeth on one side of the lower jaw. State their names and uses. Give diagram of a longitudinal section of a simple tooth, with names of its parts.

2. Give outline diagram of the neck and trunk, with names of the regions. Insert outline of alimentary canal, with names of its parts, and show relative position of the stomach and diaphragm.

3. What is the diaphragm? Give outline diagram indicating condition of diaphragm before and after inspiration.

4. State digestive actions of pancreatic juice. Which of them is peculiar? Name some uses of the liver.

5. Of what is the heart chiefly composed? Give diagram of left side of heart, showing relative thickness of walls, the position of the vessels and valves, and naming all the parts. Give diagram of cross-section of heart about midway between base and apex.

ARITHMETIC.

1. Define: an abstract number, prime factors, quotient, mixed number, cube root, percentage, bank discount, compound interest.

2. Get sum of five, five tenths, thirty-seven thousandths, one thousand millionths, XIX, MDCCCLX, XXI, .18.

3. Find all the common divisors of 225, 2025, 8100.

4. Divide $\frac{4}{5}$ of 91 by $\frac{10}{27}$ of 637.

5. What is the amount at comp. interest of $500 for 2 y. 6 m. at 7 per cent.?

6. Get square root of 530 to three decimal places and give reasons for the several steps in the work.

7. Give common and metric table of liquid measure.

8. How many litres in 10 gal. 3 qt. 1 pt. 3 gil., the gallon being 231 cu. in. and the metre 36.37 in.

PLANE GEOMETRY.

1. Define: an axiom, a point, a right angle, two parallel lines, a

polygon, the apothegm of a regular polygon, a circle, a tangent to a circle, the area of a surface, a commensurable ratio.

Draw an obtuse angled triangle; then draw the three altitudes, taking the three sides of the triangle in turn as bases.

2. If two sides of one triangle be respectively equal to two sides of another, but if the included angle in the first be greater than the included angle in the second triangle, the third side of the first triangle is greater than the third side of the second.

3. A straight line perpendicular to a radius at its extremity is tangent to the circle, and conversely.

4. In any triangle, if a straight line be drawn from the vertex to the middle of the base, then :

(1) The sum of the squares of the two sides is equal to twice the square of half the base increased by twice the square of the medial line.

(2) The difference of the squares of the two sides is equal to twice the product of the base by the distance from the middle of the base to the foot of the perpendicular from the vertex to the base.

5. The area of a trapezoid is equal to the product of its altitude by half the sum of its parallel sides.

If the area of a trapezoid be 80 square yards, the perpendicular 4 yards, and one of the parallel sides 15 yards ; what is the other parallel side ?

6. To construct the mean proportional between two lines.

ALGEBRA.

1. Define: known and unknown quantities, positive and negative quantities, addition, a common multiple of two or more numbers, a radical, an equation, a theorem.

2. Resolve $m^4 - n^4$ into three prime factors.

3. Reduce the fraction $\dfrac{\sqrt{(x^2 + xy + y^2)}}{\sqrt{(x-y)}}$ to an equivalent fraction having a rational denominator.

4. Divide $x + y + z - 3\sqrt[3]{xyz}$ by $x^{\frac13} + y^{\frac13} + z^{\frac13}$.

5. For $8 I can buy 2 lbs. of tea, 10 lbs. of coffee, and 20 lbs. of sugar, or 3 lbs. of tea, 5 lbs. of coffee, and 30 lbs. of sugar, or 5 lbs of tea, 5 lbs. of coffee, and 10 lbs. of sugar. What are the prices ?

6. Solve the equation

$$\frac{ax-b}{4} + \frac{a}{3} = \frac{bx}{2} - \frac{bx-a}{3}.$$

7. Solve the equation $x+5+ \sqrt{(x+5)}=6$, giving all the roots.

8. Solve the equation

$$\frac{x+a}{x-2a} + \frac{x-2a}{x+a} = 1,$$

and get the sum, and the product, of the two roots.

LATIN.

1. Translate Cæsar, B. G., V., 9.

Give reason for mood and tense of *consedissent, essent;* for case of *navibus* (before *essent*), *navibus* (before *quod*). Give principal parts of *cognovit* and *veritus*, and inflect the former in future indicative active, the latter in imperfect subjunctive. What is the positive of the adverb *minus ?*

2. Translate Virgil, Ecl. X., 70–77.

Who was Gallus, and what his fate?
Where did pastoral poetry originate?
How is the tense of *venit* to be determined?

3. Translate Æneid, IV., 238–244.

Who is *ille ?* What is the special name of this *virga ?* Explain derivation of *imperio, talaria, rapido, flamine,* giving prefix, root, and ending employed to form stem from root, with meaning of each of these parts.

Give principal parts of *parere* and *parabat,* and mark quantity of each syllable. Write out last two verses above, dividing into feet and marking caesuras, and give rules for length of all penultimate and final syllables. Indicate by English spelling the Roman pronunciation of the verse *dixerat,* etc.

4. Translate Cic. in Cat. III., 28.

Of what kind is the condition *si verterit ?* Explain mood and tense of *lubeat ?*

What two opinions were advocated in the senate (fourth oration) in regard to the punishment of the conspirators, and by whom were these opinions represented? Which did Cicero support?

5. TRANSLATE AT SIGHT :—

[Sulla is accused by Torquatus, the son of a former rival, of complicity in the conspiracy of Catiline.]

Hic tu epistulam meam saepe recitas, quam ego ad Cn. Pompeium de meis rebus gestis et de summa re publica misi, et ex ea crimen aliquod in P. Sullam quaeris ; et si furorem incredibilem biennio ante conceptum erupisse in meo consulatu scripsi, me hoc demonstrasse dicis, Sullam in illa fuisse superiore conjuratione. . . . . . . De quo etiam si quis dubitasset antea num id, quod tu arguis, cogitasset, interfecto patre tuo consulem descendere Kalendis Ianuariis cum lictoribus, sustulisti hanc suspicionem, cum dixisti hunc, ut Catilinam consulem efficeret, contra patrem tuum operas et manum comparasse.

Explain construction of *scripsi, dubitasset, descendere, biennio*.

GREEK.

[Translate any *two* of the following passages, and answer *all* the questions. Write all Greek words with their proper accents.]

1. Xenophon, Anab. IV., 3.20.

Give nom., acc. and gen. sing. of σκευῶν, ὄρεσιν, χεῖρας. Principal parts of ὁρῶντες, ᾤχοντο, ἐπιδραμεῖν, φεύγειν? On what root is θᾶττον formed and how? Compare ὀλίγους, πολλοί.

2. Xenophon, Hellenica II., 2.16.

Decline εἰδώς, πλείω through the sing. Give first ten cardinal numerals in Greek.

By whose advice were the Long Walls of Athens built? What purpose did they serve? By whom were they finally restored?

3. Xenophon, Lacedæmonian Const., VII., 1.

4. Write in Greek :—

[Most of the Greek words may be found in the second prose-passage above.]

The Athenians would not have sent Theramenes, if they had supposed that he would stay three months with Lysander. For they knew their provisions were likely to fail them in that time.

5. Translate Iliad, II., 474-483.

Where formed (tense, mood, voice), and from what verbs, are μιγέωσιν and ἀγρομένῃσιν? Give their *Attic* forms.

6. Translate Il., III., 191-202.

Explain accent of ὥς (6). Scan last two lines.

AMHERST.

[REQUIREMENTS FOR ADMISSION: The College permits the student to choose one of two courses in Latin and Greek. The following requirements have been selected as the least difficult: *Greek*, Grammar, Prose Composition (Jones's), *Anabasis*, IV Books, *Iliad*, III Books. *Latin*, Grammar, Prose Composition (Ilkness.), Seven Orations of Cicero, including the Pro Lege Manilia, Æneid, VI Books, Cæsar Books I-IV., Eclogues of Virgil and the first two Georgics. *Mathematics:* Arithmetic Complete; Algebra through Quadratics, including Radicals, Geometrical and Arith. Progressions, Binomial Theorem, and Proportion; Plané Geometry. *English:* Composition and Correction of false syntax. *French:* Keetel's Elementary Grammer. *Ancient History* and outlines of Gk. and Roman Geog.]

(1882).

GREEK.

1. Translate Iliad I. 245-253.

2. Translate Iliad II. 1-7.

3. Translate Iliad III. 320-327.

4. Write the nom. sg. of ἤλοισι, μέλιτος. Decline in Attic forms ἀνέρες, πολέας, νηυσίν, ἔπεα.

5. Compare γλυκίων, ἀρίστη, κίδιστε, μέγιστε.

6. Using Attic forms, (*a*) Inflect φάτο, ρ'έεν (with contractions), τράφεν, ἐγένοντο : (*b*) Synopsis of βάλε, τράφεν, ἐγένοντο, ἔθηκεν (including sec. aor. forms), δός, δῦναι : (*c*) Principal parts of φάτο, βάλε, ἐγένοντο, ἔχε, φαίνετο. What is the tense and the analysis of the form ἔφαν?

7. Name the enclitics in the second passage ; and account for the accent of δ' (2) and ἐπ' (6).

8. State the derivation, and the force of the derivative suffixes, of Πηλείδης, σκῆπτρον, ἑτέρωθεν, ἀγορητής, φιλότητα ; the composition of ἡδυεπής, ἱπποκορυσταί, παννύχιοι, Ἀγαμέμνονι, ἀερσίποδες.

9. Syntax of ἤλοισι, τοῖσι, μέλιτος, τῷ (6), οἱ (7).

10. Write any four lines metrically divided.

11. Where were Pylus and Ida ? Give a short analysis of Book III.

(ANABASIS).

1. Translate Anab. I. 3.,8.
    Anab. II. 3.,18.
    Anab. III. 1.,43.
    Anab. IV. 2.,18.19.

2. Syntax of every genitive and infinitive ; and give exact meaning of every preposition here found with a genitive.

3. Put into Greek : And Menon also after having taken his javelins into his hands, mounted his horse.—On the following day, Cyrus sent for your soldiers to come to him. For Cyrus had been appointed general in place of his brother. I asked what they were doing ; and he replied that they were riding at full speed. If any one had gone into the city, what would he have suffered ? He answered that if you had not come, we should be marching.

LATIN.

1. Translate Cæsar B. G.

2. State how much Cæsar you have read and reviewed.

3. Give the principal parts of *cognoscenda, revertatur, proficiscitur.* and *trajectus.*

4. Explain all the *subjunctives* in the above passage.

5. When is *quod* followed by the subjunctive ?

6. Translate Cicero.

7. State how much Cicero you have read and reviewed.

8. Explain the difference in the use of *gratia* with the verbs *agere, habere* and *referre.*

9. Explain the use of the ablative case in *verbis, virtute, jure* and *consiliis.*

(FOR TRANSLATION AT SIGHT).

10. At enim haec ita commissa sunt ab isto, ut non cognita sint ab hominibus ? Hominem arbitror esse neminem. qui nomen istius audierit, quin facta quoque ejus nefaria commemorare possit ; ut mihi magis timendum sit, ne multa crimina praetermittere, quam ne qua in istum fingere, existimer. Neque enim mihi videtur haec multitudo, quae ad audiendum convenit, cognoscere ex me causam voluisse, sed ea quae scit, mecum recognoscere.

(VIRGIL).

1. Translate Æneid, IV. 129-142.

2. Divide lines 2, 7, 8, 9 into feet and mark place of cæsural pause in each.

3. Write out rule or rule and exception, for the quantity of syllables whose vowels are in italics : as, Oce*a*num, *i*nterea, A*u*rora, port*i*s, jub*a*re, l*a*to, equ*i*tes, od*o*ra, pr*i*mi.

4. Write rule for quantity of final vowels ; of *i* and *e* in the increments of conjugation.

5. State the outline of Bk. IV., and how the passage selected is related to it.

6. Translate Eclogue II., 27-39.

7. Translate Georgics, 287-296.

(LATIN COMPOSITION).

Translate into Latin:—

Rome was saved by a man of the greatest wisdom,—Cicero. Having been elected consul at a time when the state was in extreme peril, he did everything possible for the sake of defending the city. First of all, ambassadors were sent to Cæsar to say that the conspirators had left the city for the camp of Manlius, and that Catiline had been made leader. Then, he asked the senators what they thought ought to be done. The citizens were ordered to defend the temples of the gods and their own homes. All these things which had been commanded were done promptly and bravely. There were some who seemed uninterested, but the greater part were eager to aid the consul. Pompey, Scipio, and Cæsar conquered the enemy in two battles, and having persuaded them to surrender, at length freed the state from danger. The soldiers, to whom the safety of their country was dearer than life, were worthy of the highest praise. A vote of thanks (gratiæ) to Cicero was passed (ago) in the most honorable words because the republic had been delivered from the greatest perils by his wisdom and prudence. Then Pompey was deservedly praised, whose assistance the consul had employed. A thanksgiving was decreed to the immortal gods on Oct. 21st, which was celebrated at Rome with great rejoicing.

ANCIENT HISTORY.

1. Divisions of Greece.
2. Physical character of Attica.
3. Occasion and main events of the Persian War.
4. Work and character of Pericles.
5. Epaminondas.
6. Physical character of Italy.
7. Situation of Etruria and Latium.
8. Occasion of the First Punic War.
9. Marius and Sulla.
10. Augustus.

(ENGLISH).

Write a composition on one of the following subjects:—

1. The occasion, argument, character and result of Othello's defence before the Duke of Venice and his council.

2. A description of the gaol in which the Vicar of Wakefield was confined, and of his life during his imprisonment.

3. The character of Iago.

4. Correct the following sentences :—

(a). One's education always influence their opinions.

(b). "Things bad begun make strong themselves by ill."

(c). "I have a mind to inquire after one thing,—the which you can easily satisfy me in."

(d). The library should have been catalogued. Its omission makes the books most entirely useless.

(e). We all planned to have gone home in the evening, but the shower surprised us before sunset, and each one got away as quick as they possibly could.

(f). It was quite a ways to the city, and the troops tired before entering it.

(g). There were thirteen persons set at the table, and some argued misfortune from this event, yet it was requested that none would leave their seats during dinner.

(h). There were some ten or twelve agriculturalists who awarded the prizes.

ARITHMETIC.

(1.) Give the rule for dividing one vulgar fraction by another. Give the reason of the rule and illustrate by an example.

(2.) What part of $\dfrac{3\frac{4}{3}}{\frac{2}{7}}$ of a rod is $\frac{2}{3}$ of an inch.

(3.) How many feet in a fence enclosing an acre in the form of a square?

(4.) Find the value of $\dfrac{0.1 \times 0.002}{0.0001 \times 200} + \frac{3}{6}$.

(5.) How many cords of wood can be put into a space 20.5 feet long, 12.75 feet wide, and 7.6 feet high?

(6.) Find the square root of 0.8 to 3 places.

(7.) What is the present worth of $678.75, due 3 years 7 months hence, at $7\frac{1}{2}$ per cent.?

(8.) If 16 horses consume 84 bushels of grain in 24 days, how many bushels will suffice 32 horses 48 days?

[NOTE.—The examination in Plane Geometry is conducted orally.]

ALGEBRA.

(1.) Reduce $\dfrac{x^{2n}-y^{2n}}{x^n+y^n}$ to its lowest terms.

(2.) Find a number of two digits such that it shall be equal to 7 times the sum of its digits, and if 27 be subtracted from the number, the digits will be inverted.

(3.) Reduce $4\sqrt{2}-6\sqrt{8}+10\sqrt{32}$ to its simplest form.

(4.) Extract the square root of $81\ a^4\ x^{-2}\ y^{\frac{2}{3}}\ z^{-\frac{1}{5}}$.

(5.) Solve the equation $3\ x^2-4\ x=119$.

(6.) Form a quadratic equation whose roots shall be -3 and -2.

(7.) Solve the equations, $\begin{cases} y^2 + xy = 15. \\ x^2 + xy = 10. \end{cases}$

(8.) What proportions may be derived from the proportion $a:b::c:d$?

(9.) Find the sum of the first n odd numbers $1+3+5\ldots 2n-1$.

(10.) What is the sum of the infinite descending series $\frac{1}{3}+\frac{1}{3}{}^2_2+\frac{1}{3}{}^3$ + etc.?

(11.) Give the first four terms of $(1+2\ x^2)^n$.

FRENCH.

I. Give the rule respecting the pronunciation of final consonants.

2. What nouns take x in the plural ?

3. Give the feminine form of *bon, nouveaux, sec, doux, faux*.

4. State the distinction between the possessive adjectives and the possessive pronouns, and give examples of each.

5. Give the primitive tenses (principal parts) of *couvrir, devoir, écrire, lire, naître, savoir, tenir*, and conjugate the present tense of each verb.

6. Synopsis of *finir*, simple tenses.

II. Translate into French :—

I was giving ; he gave ; they will give ; he might have given ; let us give. Has your brother taken a walk this morning? He has not taken a walk, for he did not go to bed till eleven o'clock, and he has not yet risen. What time is it now ? It is a quarter past eight. His sister needs some money, will you lend her some ? I would lend her some if I had any. Do you think of your friends ? I think of them. When did Charlemagne die ? He died on the twenty-eighth of January, 814. Peter the Great died at St. Petersburgh the eighth day of February, 1725.

III. Translate into English :—

Il y a très-longtemps que nous ne nous sommes vus. Nous nous promenions tous les jours sur les boulevards. J'écrivis chez moi le lendemain de mon arrivée à Paris. Puisque vous le désirez je remettrai ce voyage à demain. Je suis content pourvu que vous le soyez. Il y a des hommes qui sont toujours mécontents. Dans une bataille où les boulets ennemis volaient autour de lui, Napoléon s'écria : Le boulet qui doit me tuer, n'est pas encore fondu. Si vous êtes vertueux vous serez aimés et estimes de tout le monde.

WILLIAMS.

[REQUIREMENTS FOR ADMISSION: *Greek.* Anabasis, I.–IV.; Iliad, I., II.; Prose Composition; History; Grammar. *Latin.* Cæsar, I.–IV.; Cicero, seven orations; Virgil, Georgics and Æneid, I.–IV.; Prose Composition; Grammar; History. *Mathematics.* Arithmetic, complete; Algebra to Quadratics; Loomis's Geometry, I.–IV. *English Grammar. Ancient and Modern Geography.*]

ENTRANCE EXAMINATION.

1882.

GREEK.

1. Translate Iliad, II., 212–223.
Write out two lines to show feet and cæsura.

2. Translate Anab., IV., vi., 16.

3. Decline ἐγώ, παιδείαν, ὄρος, κλωπῶν, βουσίν.

4. Give the principal parts of ἀκούω, ἐπιδείκνυμι, ἔχω, λαμβάνω.

5. Give the synopsis of εἶναι, δειπνήσωμεν, ἔλαβον, ἔσται.

6. Inflect ἀξιοῦνται (giving both uncontracted and contracted forms), λάβωμεν, ἔσται.

7. The construction of κλέπτειν, κινδύνου, τῷ κλέπτοντι, τούτων, βατά?

8. Translate into Greek (a vocabulary of the different words being given):—

But when-now[1] they were crossing[2] the mountains, the peltasts[3] running-ahead[4] perceived[5] the encampment[6] of the enemy and did not wait-for[7] the hoplites. And the barbarians having heard the uproar[8] did not stand-their-ground,[9] but fled.[10] And when the hoplites learned[11] of this, it seemed best to them to retire[12] to their camp lest[13] the barbarians should-attack[14] the guards[15] left[16] [there].

9. Translate at sight :—

Οἱ δὲ στρατιῶται τότε μὲν δειπνήσαντες καὶ φυλακὰς καταστησάμενοι καὶ συσκευασάμενοι πάντα ἃ ἔδει ἐκοιμήθησαν. ἡνίκα δ' ἦν ἐν μέσῳ νυκτῶν, ἐσήμηνε τῷ κέρατι. Κῦρος δ' εἰπὼν τῷ Ἀρυσάντᾳ ὅτι ἐπὶ τῇ ὁδῷ ὑπομένοι ἐν τῷ πρόσθεν τοῦ στρατεύματος ἐξήει λαβὼν τοὺς ἀμφ' αὐτὸν ὑπηρέτας· βραχεῖ δὲ χρόνῳ ὕστερον Ἀρυσάντας παρῆν ἄγων τοὺς θωρακοφόρους.

10. Give a brief account (with dates) of Pausanias and Lysander; of Miltiades and Pericles.

11. Mention the states which successively had a dominating nfluence in Greek affairs from 490 to 323 B. C., with the dates.

12. Where were Sphacteria, Plataea, Aegospotami, Leuctra? For what were they famous? Dates? •

LATIN.

1. Translate Cic., pro Arch., 10.

Explain fully construction of esset, civitate, donaretur, donaret, repudiasset, scriberet. Derivation of *epigramma, vendebat?*

2. Translate Virg. Georg., IV., 88–94.

3. Translate Æneid, III., 497–505.

Explain fully the construction of *revocaveris, obsit, neci, regnet, maculis,* in 2; of *fuerit, cernam, epiro, maneat,* in 3. Mark the metre of the last line of 3. What is the subject of the fourth Georgic? Who is the speaker in the third book of the Æneid? When did Virgil live?

4. What was the first Roman conquest outside of Italy, and when was it made? What was their first conquest out of Europe, and when was it made? What was the office of Tribune of the People, and how and when was it established? Tell where each of the following places is, and what event of Roman history is connected with it :—Cannæ, Heraclea, Zama, Actium, Thapsus, Philippi, Numantia.

5. Translate at sight, Cæsar, B. G., VIII., 49.

6. Translate into Latin :—

Cæsar wintered in Belgium, in order that the states might be kept in friendship. He knew[1] *how*[2] *important it was* that he *be* always *present,*[3] and feared[4] that his departure might be the signal[5] to the Gauls of renewing[6] the war. The province *was* always *within*[7] *a little* of *revolting.*[8] The Senate *decreed*[9] that Cæsar dismiss[10] his troops.

1 intellegere; 2 quanti interesse; 3 adesse; 4 vereri; 5 signum; 6 renovare; 7 minimum abesse; 8 deficere; 9 decernere; 10 dimittere. •

ENGLISH.

I. Write a composition upon one of the following subjects : The Story of the Caskets ; Shylock ; The Holy Grail.

II. Criticise the following sentences :—

I would be foolish, if I did not agree to it.

I don't remember of having heard it.

Will we come to-morrow?

You must not learn me to remember any extraordinary pleasure.

He only advised me to go.

I am not bound to receive any messenger that you send.

Before the telescope was discovered, the observance of the heavenly bodies was difficult, and the astronomers often failed to produce complete persuasion.

He did not like him so well as his colleagues.

I expected to have found him.

William Shakespeare was the sun among the lesser lights of English poetry, and a native of Stratford-on-Avon.

ARITHMETIC.

1. Write in figures, nine billions two hundred millions forty thousand and seven.

2. What is the sum of $\frac{3}{8}$, $9\frac{1}{2}$, and $\frac{1}{4}$ of $\frac{2}{3}$?

3. Reduce $\frac{14}{27}$ to a decimal, and extract the square root to three places.

4. What is the interest of $1047.50 from June 1, 1875, to June 25, 1882, at 7 per cent.?

5. What must be the length of a bin 1.53 metres wide, and 1.27 metres deep, to hold 100 hectolitres?

GEOMETRY.

1. Find the sum of all the interior angles of a polygon.

2. Two parallels intercept equal arcs of a circumference.

3. In any triangle the square of a side opposite to an acute angle equals what?

ALGEBRA.

1. Change to a fraction $x+5-\dfrac{2x-15}{x-3}$.

2. $\dfrac{5x-7}{2}-\dfrac{2x+7}{3}=3x-14$.   Find the value of x.

3. A boy who runs at the rate of 12 yards per second, starts 20 yards behind another who runs $10\frac{1}{2}$ yards per second. How soon will the first boy be 10 yards ahead of the second?

4. Multiply $\sqrt[3]{4a}$ by $\sqrt{6x}$.

5. Find the value of $\dfrac{3}{\sqrt[4]{2}}$ to three places of decimals.

[Note : The examination in Modern Geography is conducted orally.]

COLUMBIA.

[REQUIREMENTS FOR ADMISSION : *Greek.* Three books of the Iliad, Four books of the Anabasis, Hadley's Greek Grammar, Greek Prosody, Greek Prose Composition (sentences from the Anabasis).—*Latin.* Four books of Cæsar's De Bello Gallico, Eclogues of Virgil, Six Orations of Cicero, Six books of Virgil's Æneid, Latin Prosody, Prose Composition (sentences from Cicero and Cæsar), Harkness's Latin Grammar.—*English.* Grammar (Quackenbos's), Composition (an essay written off-hand during the examination).—*Ancient History* (Greece. Rome, Persia).—*Ancient Geography.*—*Modern Geography.*—*Mathematics.*—Peck's Arithmetic complete, Five books of Peck's Algebra, Four books of Davies' Legendre. The student must answer fifty per cent. of the questions asked.]

I. MATHEMATICS.

ENTRANCE EXAMINATION.

1. Add together $\frac{7}{8}$ of $\frac{3}{4}$, $\frac{7\frac{3}{5}}{2\frac{1}{4}}$, $\frac{8\frac{3}{7}}{9}$, $\frac{1}{3}$, and extract cube root of result.

2. If 3 men in 16 days of 12 hrs. each build a wall 30 ft. long, 8 ft. high, and 3 thick, how many men are required to build wall 45 ft. long, 9 ft. high, and 6 ft. thick, in 24 days of 9 hours?

3. A, B, and C enter into partnership. A puts in $\frac{1}{3}$ of the capital, B $\frac{1}{4}$ of the capital, and C the rest. At the end of the year the profits amount to $10,440. What is C's share of the profits?

4. In the metric system, what is the unit for measuring ordinary surfaces, and what is its value in common measure? Reduce 120 metres to cu. ft.

5. Find least com. mult. of x^3-1, and x^2+x-2.

6. Add $\frac{x-y}{y}$, $\frac{2x}{x-y}$, $\frac{x^3-x^2y}{x^2y-y^3}$.

7. Solve the equation $\frac{1}{2}\left(x-\frac{a}{3}\right)-\frac{1}{3}\left(x-\frac{a}{4}\right)+\frac{1}{4}\left(x-\frac{a}{5}\right)=0$.

8. Prove what the sum of 3 angles of a plane triangle are equal to.

9. Define an inscribed angle, and prove what its measure equals.

10. Prove that similar polygons may be divided into the same number
*riangles similarly situated each to each, and similarly placed.

FRESHMAN CLASS.
1879.

1. What is the sum of the squares of two sides of a triangle equal to?

2. When will two plane triangles be equal in all parts?

3. When will two plane triangles be similar?

4. Given a rt. angled triangle, ABC, right angled at B. AC=h and
AB : BC :: m : n. Find AB and BC.

5. Find area of octagon inscribed in circle whose radius is 1.

6. Deduce an expression for area of any circle in terms of the
square of its radius.

7. What determines the position of a plane?

8. Any two rectangular parallelopipedons are to each other as the
products of their three dimensions. Demonstrate.

9. Give the regular polyhedrons.

10. Give formulæ for Convex Surface and volume of cylinder, cone,
and frustum of cone.

11. R=5. Find S. and V. of a sphere.

12. Give formulæ for area of any zone, volume of any · spherical
sector and volume of any spherical segment.

13. If two triangles on the same or equal spheres are mutually equiangular, they are also mutually equilateral. Demonstrate.

14. Angle of lune=90°—find L in terms of surface of sphere taken
as a unit.

15. In spherical triangle, A=90°, B=90°, C=30°. Draw polar.

16. In spherical triangle ABC, A=20°, B=130°, C=80°. Find area
when radius of sphere=5.

17. Give expression for vol. of any spher. wedge.

18. Give ultimate syllogism to prove that vol. of any pyramid=⅓ of
product of base by altitude.

19. Why is any section of a sphere made by a plane, a circle?

20. How many and what quantities does π represent and what is
always its numerical value?

SOPHOMORE CLASS.
(Jan. 1880.)

1. Prove what the square of ordinate of any point of a parabola is
equal to.

2. Prove that the bisectrix of angle formed by one of the focal lines
of a point of the ellipse and prolongation of other focal lines, is tangent
to the curve at that point.

3. How must conic surface be cut, that the section may be a hyperbola? Demonstrate.

4. Find arc whose natural sine is .7432. Find nat. cot. of 58° 19′ 40″.

5. In a rt. angled plane triangle, b=152.67 yds.; C=50° 18′ 32″. Find a.

6. In rt. angled plane triangle, b=103.65; c=101.22; solve the triangle. ·

7. In plane triangle, B=41° 28′; b=50 yds.; c=72 yds. How many values has C, and why?

8. Solve plane triangle in which a̅=74.85; b=65.84, and c=36.95.

9. Deduce relations between circular functions of any arc.

10. Deduce values of sin (a+b) and cos (a+b).

(Monthly Examination: Feb., 1880.)

1. $\dfrac{\text{Sin } p - \text{sin } q}{\text{sin } (p-q)} = \dfrac{\text{sin } (p+q)}{\text{sin } p + \text{sin } q}$.

Deduce, and demonstrate use.

2. Name Napier's circular parts. Give rules for circular parts, and write out corresponding formulæ.

3. Prove that each side about the rt. angle in a rt. angled spherical triangle is of same species as its opposite angle.

4. Determine when the two sides about the rt. angle in a rt. angled spherical triangle are of same and when of difft. species.

(March, 1880.)

1. In a rt. angled spher. triangle, given c=29° 46′ 08″, b=155° 27′ 54″, find a and B.

2. Deduce value of sin ½ a in any spher. triangle.

3. Write out both sets of Napier's Analogies and state their use.

(Final Examination: 1879.

1. Deduce values of functions of 2 a.

2. Prove formula $\dfrac{\text{sin } p - \text{sin } q.}{\text{sin } (p-q)} = \dfrac{\text{sin } (p+q)}{\text{sin } p + \text{sin } q}$ and state its use.

3. In rt. angled spher. triangle, an oblique angle and side opposite being given, deduce rule for determining when there will be two solutions, one solution, or none.

4. In a rt. angled spher. triangle, a=86° 51′; B=18° 03′ 32″. Find c.

5. Deduce value of sin ½ a in a spher. triangle.

6. In oblique angled spher. triangle, B=42° 15′ 13″; C=121° 36′ 12″; a=40° 0′ 10″. Solve triangle.

7. Deduce rule for finding area of plane triangle when three sides are given.

8. Find entire surface of a rt. pyramid whose slant ht. is 15 ft. and its base a pentagon each side of which is 25 ft.

9. Find vol. of tetrahedron whose edge is 25 yards.

10. Describe Surveyor's Compass and state its use.

(FINAL EXAMINATION : 1880).

1. In a rt. angled spher. triangle :

(a). C=105°15′; a=75°30′ ; is b gter. or less than 90°?

(b). a=? [gter. or less than 90°] when b=85°40′ and c=78°22′.

(c). C=98°35′; c=110°17′; how many solutions and why?

(d). b=64°18′; B=70°20′; how many solutions and why?

2. In an oblique-angled sph. triangle :

(a). A=50°12′ ; B=58°08′ ; a=62°42′ : Find b and solve in blank.

(b). a=84°14′29″ ; b=44°13′45″ C=36°45′28″ : find A and B.

(c). A=109°55′42″ ; B=106°38′33″ ; C=120°43′37″ ; find c.

3. Deduce rule for area of triangle when 3 sides are given.

4. Find area of circular seg. whose chord is 12 and R of circle=10.

5. Find vol. of pentagonal pyramid, its altitude being 12 ft. and each side of base 2 ft.

6. The Y-level—its construction, adjustment, use?

JUNIOR CLASS.

(ANALYTICAL GEOMETRY: 1881).

1. Find distance from origin to intersection of lines $2y+3x+4=0$ and $3y+x-2=0$.

2. Given two circles $(x-5)^2+(y-4)^2=4$ and $(x-2)^2+(x-1)^2=1$; find point such that tangent drawn from it to circles shall be of equal length.

3. Show that tangents to any parabola at extremities of a focal chord are perpendic. to each other.

4. Find point from which equal tangents can be drawn to the circles $(x-5)^2+(y-4)^2=9$, $(x+4)^2+(y-1)^2=25$, and $(x-7)^2+(y+3)^2=16$.

5. Find equation of an ellipse referred to its centre.

6. Find equation of a tangent to the ellipse $3y^2+2x^2=35$, at a point whose abscissa is 2.

(MECHANICS: 1881).

1. Demonstrate Polygon of Forces.

2. Deduce rule of finding centre of gravity of a triangle.

3. Find conditions of equilibrium of elbow-joint press.
4. Find formula for time of vibration of simple pendulum.
5. Write out Marriotte's Law and Gay Lussac's Law.

SENIOR CLASS.

[The examinations in Astronomy are conducted orally, each student being questioned for three minutes. The following will serve as specimens of the questions generally asked].

[*Jan.*, 1881.]

Explain Axis, Zenith, Nadir, Celestial Horizon, Rational Horizon, Sensible Horizon, phenomena of parallel sphere.

On what does Horiz. Parallax depend?

Deduce formulas $\rho = \sin \pi$; and $r = \dfrac{\rho}{\sin \pi}$.

Give Kepler's three laws, and Newton's laws of motion.

Give outline of Maskelyne's method of measuring mass of earth.

[*May*, 1881.]

Explain Bode's Law. Give relative sizes, manners, distances, densities etc., of bodies of Solar System.

Explain Solar spots. Location of faculæ. Shape of nucleus. Filamentary character of penumbra. Periodicity of spots.

Give an account of variable stars. Temporary stars. Double stars
Explain Secchi's star-type spectra.

Give an outline of the probable construction of the heavens.

II. GREEK.

(ENTRANCE EXAMINATION, 1882.)

1. Translate (a) Xen. Anab. II. 5. (27, τῇ ὑστεραίᾳ ad fin.)

(b) Xen. Anab. IV. 7. (7).

2. Account for accents of ἐλθὼν, δῆλός, χρῆναι.

3. Write Nom. and Gen. Sing. of Τισσαφέρνει, Ἑλλήνων, προδότας, κακόνους, and ὄντας (of this last in all genders).

4. State where the following forms are found: ἐλθὼν, ἀπήγγελλεν, χρῆναι, ἱέναι, ὄντας. Write the principal parts of these verbs, and of διαβάλλοντες and τιμωρηθῆναι.

5. Give rules for case of ὑστεραίᾳ, οἰόμενος, Τισσαφέρνει, Ἑλλήνων, προδότας; and for mood of διακεῖσθαι, ἱέναι, ἐλεγχθῶσι. What is the subject of ἱέναι?

6. Compare δῆλος and κακόνους; also μέγας and πολύς. Give general rules for comparison of adjectives and adverbs.

7. Give rules for mood of ἀρξώμεθα, εἴη, πορενώμεθα. Compare θᾶττον.

8. (a). Translate Iliad Bk. II. 257–261.

(b). Iliad Bk. III. 216–219.

9. Write Attic for τοι, ἐρέω, τὸ, 'Οδυσῆϊ, ὡμοισιν, Τηλεμάχοιο.

10. Give rules for mood of κιχήσομαι, ἐπείη, δύσω. To what word does ἀπὸ belong, and what name is given to this arrangement?

11. στάσκεν, ἴδεσκε, and ἔχεσκεν where found? Give their Attic equivalents.

12. In what metre is the Iliad written? What feet allowed in it, with what restrictions? Define hiatus, and mention the principal devices for avoiding it.

13. Write in full the scansion of the first two lines of passage (b), and give rules for quantity of each syllable in the first line.

14. Translate into Greek, with accents : (1) Let us with the aid of the gods rescue ourselves even from these great perils. (2) If any one had gone into the city, what would he have suffered ? (3) I asked Menon for five months' pay and three thousand soldiers. (4) Cyrus having called the soldiers together, spoke these words to them. (5) And now it was about full market time, and the place where they intended to halt was fifteen furlongs distant.

[FRESHMEN : INTERMEDIATE EXAM. ODYSSEY.]

1. Translate Bk. 6, 25–35.

2. Explain the use of σιγαλόεντα. To what does line 28 refer ? What explanation may be offered in defence of line 35 ?

3. Name the elements of γείνατο, ἐννυσθαι, ἀγωνται, χαίρουσι, ἰομεν᾽ πλυνέουσαι, ἐντύνεαι.

4. Write and scan lines 30–35.

5. Name the transitive tenses of γείνομαι, βαίνω, ἴστημι.

6. Account for the case of τί, αὐτὴν, ἀνθρώπους, φαινομένηφιν, Φαιήκων, αὐτῇ.

7. Translate Bk. 6, 259–69.

8. Change all dialectic forms of these lines to their Attic equivalents.

9. Write all admissible Homeric forms for ἀγοραῖς, 'Οδυσσέως, στήθεσι, εἴ, ὤν.

10. Give fuller explanation of πύργος, εἰσίθμη, ἐπίστιον, Ποσιδήιον.

11. What have been the various interpretations of line 267, and what recent light on the question ?

12. Translate Bk. 7, 78–90.

13. Where was Scheria? What difficulty about the mention of Marathon, line 80? What explanation? What peculiarity in the form 'Αθήνην ? Who was Erechtheus ?

14. Distinguish between κῆρ and κήρ and write the genitive of each with accent.

15. What is meant by χάλκεον οὐδὸν? What is χάλκος, in Homer? What is κύανος?

16. Explain the grammatical relation of the words in line 84.

17. Translate Bk. 7, 182-198.

18. Account for the mode of εἶπω, κατακείετε, ξεινίσσομεν, ἵκηται, πάθ-
ησιν, ἐπιδήμεναι.

19. Give the derivation of μελίφρονα, ἐκίρνα, νώμησεν, ἡγήτορες, Κλῶθες·

20. Defend your selection of subject for ἐστὶν, line 194. How does the Homeric conception of the Κλῶθες compare with the latter?

21. Explain ἐπαρξάμενος, γέροντας, and illustrate the latter.

22. Translate Bk. 8, 11-23.

23. What is the peculiarity of Δεῦτ', ἄγε? What is the construction of
ἰέναι?

24. Account for the case of ξείνοιο, δέμας, βροτῶν, κεφαλῇ, τοὺς.

25. Compare πολλοὶ, μακρότερον, πάσσονα, φίλος, δεινός.

[FINAL EXAMINATION. HERODOTUS, 1881.]

1. Name the two principal dialects of the Greek language besides the Ionic, with regions in which each of these was spoken.

2. Mention principal writers using Ionic dialect. Into what periods is this dialect divided? Give approximate dates. Which form did Hdt. use? Name some points of difference between dialect of Hm. and that of Hdt.

3. In what region was Gk. prose first written and what were chief influences which caused its rise? What collective name applied to earliest prose-writers? Who was most noted of them and his date? Mention any other facts concerning him that you can.

4. Give succinct acct. of life of Hdt.

5. How is his history divided? How are separate divisions named, and what is the general subject of his work?

6. Mention in order the Persian monarchs from establishment of empire to the year 425 B.C. In whose reign did the Ionian revolt occur? Dates of beginning and end of this reign?

7. Mention chief instigator of revolt, causes which urged him to action, and principal cities which revolted. How long did rebellion last, and what event practically ended it?

8. Relate history of Histiæus as fully as you can.

9. What four subject nations furnished fleet of Persians? Name geographical position of each and of following: Bactra, Susa, Sardis, Σαρδώ, (modern name what?); Byzantium, Miletus, Ephesus, Didymi.

42 COLUMBIA COLLEGE.

Branchidæ ; Chios, Mitylene, Samos, Naxos, Tenos, Delos ; Chersonesus. Argos, Delphi, Ægina, Eretria, Carystus, Chalcis, Marathon, Plataeæ, Thebæ, Sybaris.

10. Translate vi., 9.

11. Give Attic equivalents for all Ionic forms in first six lines.

12. Define ἀπίκατο, 'Αρισταγόρεω, ἑαυτοῦ, σφι, ἱρά, ἑσσωθέντες, ἐξανδραποδιεῦνται. Explain formation of ἀπίκατο.

13. Account for construction of μὴ οὐ γένωνται, μὴ οὐκ ἐόντες (why double negatives here ?) τῶν ἀρχέων, εὖ ποιήσας οἶκον, ἀποσχίζων.

14. Translate vi., 94.

15. Define συνῆπτο, ἀποδέξας, ἐντειλάμενος, and explain construction of ὥστε ἀναμιμνήσκοντος, φλαύρως πρήξαντα τῷ στόλῳ, and ἐξανδραποδίσαντας.

16. Who are meant by Πεισιστρατιδέων, and what reason had they for this course of action? Give a brief account of expedition here mentioned.

17. Why did Persians single out Eretria for destruction? Date of second expedition by Darius against Greece?

18. Translate vi., 111.

19. Give literal meaning of πανήγυρις, and uses of word. What English word from corresponding adjective? Trace development of meaning of English word from that of the Greek?

20 What festival is doubtless meant here? Describe briefly.

21. What were the duties of Polemarch before battle of Marathon, and what at time of Hdt.? Why ten Strategi, and why is Miltiades called the tenth?

22. Translate into Greek, *with accents :*

He has long been supposing that such misunderstandings might be stopped by familiar conversations. 2. They are said to have sung and danced, when, conquered in the (well-known) battle, they were retiring. 3. It will be my care that they cut short their replies and make them briefer. 4. If greater numbers shall be collected, much of the army will be in danger of destruction. 5. And if, avoiding this, he had not spoken of the things done by himself, he would not have been able to refute the accusations. 6. They would not say we were the guests of Philip, unless it is proper to call those who do anything for hire the guests of those who hire them.

(*Special Examination for Freshman Scholarship in Greek.*)

1. Translate Odys., Bk. VI., 130-4.

2. With what exactness may this simile be allowed to apply? Give other forms for ἴμεν, ὄιεσσιν, ἔ. Account for number of δαίεται, change of case in βοσὶ, ἐλάφους, and construction of πειρήσοντα, ἐλθεῖν.

3. Translate 156-9.

4. Explain construction of λευσσόντων, ἐισοιχνεῦσαν, ἀγάγηται. Exhibit formation of σεῖο and of corresponding Attic. Also of ἐισορόωντα, ἕσπετο, ἕσσι, ἐπέεσσι.

5. Translate 200, and explain use of μὴ. Write other particles used in questions.

6. Translate 300–7.

7. Why the modes of ἡγήσαιτο, κεκίθωσι, διελθέμεν, ἵκηαι, ἰδέσθαι? What peculiarity of metre in lines 300–4? Give explanation of ἀλιπόρφυρα.

8. Translate and explain Bk. VII., 10.

9. Translate VII., 215–25.

10. Write 215 as a prohibition. Why tense ἔπλετο, ἐσθέμεναι, ἔπαθον? Explain use of ἐπὶ in 216; λίπον, 224. Why is καίπερ peculiar for Hm.? Why not Καίπερ?

SOPHOMORE CLASS.
Medea of Euripides.

1. Give principal events in life of Euripides.

2. What number of plays ascribed to him? Name those extant.

3. What quality ascribed to him by Aristotle and on what ground?

4. Give outline of plot of Medea.

5. By which of the other great dramatists is it treated?

6. In what measure is the dialogue?

7. Give tabular view of admissible feet.

8. Why called trimeter?

9. Translate vv. 1–10.

10. Give different modes of expressing a wish.

11. Where was Colchis? The Symplegades? What and why so called?

12. What do you supply with πεσεῖν—ἐρετμῶσαι?

13. Explain construction in ἀν ἔπλευσε.

14. Give story alluded to in Πελιάδας κόρας.

15. Distinguish Πηλείδης, Πήλιον, Πελίας, Πελιάς.

16. Translate vv. 184–198.

17. Construction of δέργμα? use of ἀποταυροῦνται with δ. λεαίνης?

18. Protasis to ἀν ἀμάρτοις?

19. Translate vv. 213–218.

20. Explain subjunctive in v. 214.

21. What explanations have been given of 215–216?

22. Translate 419–429.

23. What is to be supplied in 426?

24. Translate 514–520.

25. What to be supplied before ἤ in 515? Construction of ὅτῳ? difference between διδεῖν and διειδέναι? trace meanings of χαρακτήρ.

26. Translate 551–554.

27. Explain construction after comparative in 553.

28. Translate 598–606.

29. Explain γαμοῦσα in fem. of active voice.

30. Translate 672–680.

31. How may ἄπειρος and ἄζυγες be resolved?

32. Explain accent in πέρι, use of κατὰ (675); what other rendering of 679; explain πρὶν ἂν in 680.

33. Translate 733–738.

34. What objection to reading μεθεῖς in 736? What other reading in 737–9, and what change in meaning?

(1882).—Translate into Greek:—

Do not wonder at his extravagant assertion, but observe with candor what he says.

Let us not consider that we have been born to our fathers and mothers only, but also to our native land.

They were not ashamed to declare that we had hindered the city from making peace, in addition to having been a cause of the war.

MEMORABILIA OF XENOPHON, (1877).

1. Give brief outline of life of Xen. with title of works.

2. Subject of Memorabilia? Greek name?

3. Translate the first sentence of the Memorabilia.

4. To what class of words does ending—ακις belong?

5. For what is τίσι here used?

6. What is force of ποτὲ here? Why its accent?

7. εἴη why in optative?

8. What was the indictment against Socrat. (in Greek)?

9. Translate I. i. 3. from ὁ δὲ οὐδὲν to θυσίαις.

10. For what is τῶν ἄλλων here used?

11. What is meant by οἰωναῖς, φήμαις, συμβολοις, and θυσίαις?

12. Difference in signif. and govt. between χράω and χρίομαι, γρίφω and γρίφομαι, πείθω and πείθομαι?

13. Translate I. 10, 11, to ἤκουσεν.

14. Compare πρωί; give forms of pres. inf. and imp. indic. of εἰμί, εἶμι, ἵημι.

15. Describe the περίπατοι and γυμνάσια.

16. Why is πληθούσης ἀγορᾶς in genitive? What time of day was it?
17. Explain genit. Σωκράτους πράττοντος. What is οἱ βουλόμενοι equivalent to?
18. Translate I. ii. 12.
19. Who is meant by ὁ κατήγορος? Derivation of word?
20. What name often applied to body of which Critias was a member?
21. When established in Athens? When and by whom expelled?
22. Compare πλεονεκτίστατος and give similar forms.
23. Translate I. vi., 7, to φέρουσιν.
24. Give construction of φύσει, σώματι, κρείττους, ἄν.
25. Translate I. ii. 41.
26. Difference between εἶπέ and εἶπε? Why is φάναι in infin.? Account for difference in vocative of Περίκλεις and Σώκρατες above.
27. What is force of ἔχω with an infin.? What the usage of article with proper names?
28. Explain ἂν τυχεῖν. What the subject and what the force of participle?
29. Put the words in form of direct hypothetical sentence.
30. Translate I. vi. 5. from ἢ τὴν δίαιταν to μοι ἃ ἐγώ.
31. Translate I. iv. 12, 13, and 14 to πλέον οὐδὲν ἔχει.
32. Why ζώων in genitive? ἀνθρώπων why? στόματος why? On what does ἀρθροῦν depend? What is proper subject to εἰσί? To what does ἄν after βόος belong?
33. What form of condition is βοὸς ἂν ἔχων κ. τ. λ.? Give it in full.
34. Translate II. i. 21.
35. Who was Prodicus? Give summary of the σύγγραμμα.

EXAMINATION FOR SOPHOMORE SCHOLARSHIP IN GK., 1879.

Medea of Euripides.

1. Give account of Argonautic expedition and trace course of Jason from starting place to Colchis.
2. What is the prologue to a Gk. play?
3. The dialogue in what measure? First address of Chorus in what? Choral songs how divided? What were most common measures?
4. What feet admissible in anapæstic verse?
5. What is proper ending of an anapæstic system? Define it; what common ending of choriambic system?
6. Define iambus, trochee, tribrach, amphibrach, amphimacer

molossus, dactyl, cretic, choriambus, bacchius, penthemimeris, glyconic, pherecratic.

7. Define a dochmius and give the usual variations.

8. Translate and scan vv. 148-159.

9. Where is ἀῖες found, and what forms of the verb are in use?

10. What other reading for ἐννέταν and on what ground proposed?

11. Translate 819-845.

12. For what is οὖν here? Difference between κἀν and κἂν? Tense of ἔφυς? Explain subj. λέξης.

13. Explain application of 'Ερεχθεῖδαι.

14. Different legend of Μοῦσαι and use of φυτεἰω?

15. Translate 1136-1140.

16. Explain periphrasis in first line.

17. Give forms of ἤσθημεν, and ἐσπεῖσθαι.

18. Translate 1151-1155.

19. Explain construction of οὐ μή, showing to what words the negatives extend, and of ἐμὴν χάριν.

20. Scan 1251-1260 and translate 1251-1270.

21. Construction of 1268-70.

22. How many constitute the chorus entire, and how divided?

23. Translate 1361-1375.

24. Translate 1415 to the end.

25. Of what other plays of Eurip. do these verses form the conclusion? What is the usual ending of a Gk. tragedy?

JUNIOR CLASS.

ELECTRA OF SOPHOCLES.

1. Give dates of birth and death of Sophocles.

2. Number of plays ascribed to him and number of first and second prizes awarded him?

3. Give outline of plot of the Electra.

4. Translate 42-54.

5. Explain usage of οὐ...μή (42).

6. Explain forms χρῶ, ὁθουνεκα, κυλισθείς, ἐστάτω, ἐφίετο, ἠρμένοι.

7. Derivation or composition of τροχηλάτων, δίφρων, καράτομοις, ἀψορρον.

8. Explain allusion in 45; describe custom in 52.

9. Translate 121-127.

10. Explain construc. of Αγαμέμνονα in 125.

11. Translate 147-152.

12. Explain story alluded to in 148 and 150-152.

13. Translate 244-250.

14. Explain forms ἐι κείσεται...ἔρροι ἂν.

15. Translate 387-391.

16. Translate 563-569.

17. Subject of ἔσχε? κείνης why in gen.? Why not lawful?

18. Constructions and renderings possible in 568-9?

19. Translate 680-687.

20. Name principal games of Greece, where celebrated, in whose honor?

21. Length of race course? For what is τάφεσει?

22. Translate 743-748.

23. How were the horses arranged? Distinguishing epithets? What implied in κάμπτοντος? What meant by ἐξ ἀντίγων? By τμητοῖς ἱμᾶσι? Describe fully.

24. Translate 1017-1020.

25. Translate 1058-1068.

ŒDIPUS COLONEUS (1881).

1. Give brief outline of plot of the Œdipus Rex.

2. Give the plot of Œdipus Coloneus.

3. Give a brief outline of the plot of the Antigone.

4. Translate the first Hypothesis?

5. How many plays did Sophocles write?

6. What improvements did he introduce in dramatic performances.

7. What is meant by the prologue in a Greek play? in what metre?

8. The first address of the chorus usually in what metre?

9. What was the chorus, and of whom composed?

10. Write out a scheme of iambic trimeter?

11. What is an anapæst, choriambus, tribrach, cretic, dochmius?

12. What kinds of verse are scanned by dipodies?

13. What is meant by catalectic, acatalectic, brachycatalectic, penthemimeris, logaœdic?

14. Translate vv. 36 to 52.

15. Construction of πρίν (in 36 and 48), τοῦ (in v. 38), ἱλεῳ (in 44), ὧν (in 50)?

16. Who are meant by ἐμφοβοι θεαί (39)? and give the names by which they were known.

17. Give the story of their settlement in Attica.

18. Translate vv. 311 to 323.

19. Construction of πρόσωπα, νιν (314), φῶ (315 and 317), φαιδρά (319), ὑρᾶν (322)?

20. Explain the allusion in Αἰτναίας, κυνῇ, Θεσσαλίς.

21. Translate vv. 495 to 509.

22. Explain construction of δυοῖν κακοῖν (496), ἀρκεῖν (698), the condition of v. 501, τελοῦσα, Χρήσται, τὸν τόπον.

23. Compare the characters of Antigone and Ismene as represented by Sophocles.

24. Translate vv. 668 to 693.

25. What peculiar circumstance attaches to this ode? What place is celebrated and to what is the happy condition attributed?

26. Translate vv. 835 to 847.

27 Construction of μωμένου Χεροῖν μαχεῖ; to what does ταῦτ' (v. 338). to whom does ὑμεῖς refer? (v. 847).

28. Translate vv. 1044 to 1064.

29. Explain allusion in ἐπιστροφαί, Πιθίαις, λαμπήσιν, πότνιαι, κλῆς ἐπὶ γλώσσᾳ, νιφάδος, Οἰάτιδος.

30. Translate vv. 1285 to 1307.

PROTAGORAS OF PLATO. (1882)

1. Give a brief outline of the life and writings of Plato.

2. What distribution or classification of the dialogues has been made?

3. Give a summary of the life of Socrates.

4. From what sources do we learn his philosophical opinions?

5. Give some account of the Greek Sophists as a cla s, and more particularly of those introduced in the Protagor as.

6. Give an outline of the subject of the Protagoras. and especially of the positions of the two principal speakers.

7. Translate Ch. I.

8. Explain the usage of φαίνει, ἢ δῆλα δή, ὡς...εἰρῆσθαι and similar expressions τί οὐ διηγήσω.

9. Translate Ch. IX. to D.

10. Explain the construction of ἐπεὶ κἂν σὺ....(in B), and ὥσπερ ἂν εἰ ....(in B), and such forms as Ἡρακλεώτου, and fill up (in C) what is omitted in ὅτι πρὸς γραφικήν.

11. Translate Ch. XV. to B.

12. More usual form for ἐπειδὰν θᾶττον; explain τὰ μὲν ποίει, and ἐὰν μὲν ἐκὼν πείθηται.

13. Translate Ch. XXI. (334) near bottom of p. 293.

14. What does ἐνταῦθα (end of B.) refer to? explain the form ἀλλ' ἦ; construction of σμικροτάτῳ, ὅσον μόνον?

15. Translate Ch. XXII., p. 296, first line to end of chapter.

16. Explain δολιχόδρομοι, ἡμερόδρομοι; construction of ἐμαυτοῦ.

17. Translate Ch. XXVI. to D.

18. What were the subjects of study in the Greek schools for boys?

19. Give some account of Simonides and of this poem.

20. What was the opinion of Socrates about the poets?

21. Translate Ch. XXXIV. (350 C) to 351.

22. Explain τοὺς δὲ ἀνδρείους....ὀρθῶς ὡμολόγησα.

23. What is the construction of (αὐτοὶ) αὐτῶν and ἤπριν μαθεῖν?

24. Translate Ch. XXXVII. to E.

SENIOR CLASS.

Agamemnon of Æschylus.

1. Give briefly life of Æschylus.

2. Number of plays ascribed to him, and names of those extant.

3. What is meant by trilogy; by a tetralogy?

4. Name the Orestean trilogy and their connection; the tetralogy to which the Agamemnon belonged; date of exhibition.

5. Give an outline of the plot of the Agamemnon.

6. Translate vv. 12–19.

7. What is the apodosis to εὖτ' ἂν?

8. What is the allusion in ἐντέμνων?

9. Translate vv. 33–37.

10. Explain allusion in vv. 33 and 36.

11. Translate vv. 104–120.

12. Explain κίριος as contrasted with preceding, and construction in vv. 105–107, δίθρονον κράτος, and double allusion in vv. 112–114, and in 119, and construction in 120.

13. Translate vv. 144–155.

14. What allusion in vv. 146 and 147? and explain τεκτόνα σίμφυτον.

15. Translate vv. 173–178.

16. What is the construction of ἐπινίκια? of πάθη μάθος?

17. Translate vv. 239–246.

18. Explain ὡς ἐν γραφαῖς and τριτόσπονδον.

19. Translate vv. 310–314.

20. Give the names of the signal stations and the positions of each.

21. Explain the meaning of ἄπαππον 'Ἰδ. πυρός, and λαμπάδ. νόμοι.

22. What other construction and sgnf. of v. 314?

23. Translate vv. 475-484.

24. Translate vv. 795-804.

25. Construction of λαθεῖν in v. 796?

26. Translate vv. 821-828.

27. Explain 'A. δάκος, ἵππου νεοσσός, and Πλειάδων δίσιν.

PROMETHEUS VINCTUS OF ÆSCHYLUS.

1. What plays ascribed to Æschylus on the subject of Prometheus, with their order and the subject of each?

2. Give outline of plot of Prometheus Vinctus more fully?

3. How many speakers allowed on the stage, by Æschylus and by Sophocles.

4. How many actors required to perform the play, and same actors could take what parts in it?

5. What is meant by prologue? and where does the prologue of this play end?

6. What metre usually employed in entrance song of chorus?

7. Give the admissible feet in choriambic verse.

8. Give the admissible feet in anapæstic verse.

9. What is the regular completion of an anapæstic system?

10. What measures are scanned by two feet to a metre?

11 What are the usual forms of choriambic verse? and in what does a system often end?

12. Define dactyl, spondee, iambus, trochee, cretic, anapæst, amphibrach, antispast, choriambus, pæon, epitrite, Ionic a minore, Ionic a majore, dochmius?

13. In v. 2 other reading for ἄβατον, in v. 3 explain position of δέ and construction of σοί and ἐπιστολας.

14. In v. 10 explain ὡς ἂν with subj., in v. 12 constr. of σφῷν.

15. In v. 14 συγγενῆ may refer to actual relationship; what was it?

16. Derivation of ἐξωραΐζειν (17), σταθευτός (22) ἄσμενος (23), ποικιλείμων (24), πάχνην and ἐῴαν (25), λωφήσων (27).

17. Different legends implied in Θέμιδος.

18. Translate vv. 114-127.

19. Scan vv. 128-135.

20. Translate vv. 152-159.

21. Explain construction of ὡς with indic. mood in v. 156-7.

22. What Miltonic expression suggested by 158?

23. Usual constr. of πρίν and reason for constr. in vv. 165 and 176.

24. Scan vv. 171–178 and name and define the last line.

25. Translate vv. 197–208.

26. Explain ὡς with subj. in 202 and with opt. in 203, and what reading proposed in former.

27. Translate vv. 462–468.

28. In v. 465 what objections to γένωνθ' and what substitute would avoid them?

29. Translate vv. 500–506.

30. What to be supplied with οὐδείς and what expresses the condition?

31. Scan v. 526–535.

32. How is optative used in vv. 527–532, and diff. in pres. and aor?

33. Scan vv. 574–588.

34. In v. 627 and in v. 787 explain the use of μὴ οὐ.

35. Translate vv. 707–731.

36. Give generally the course of Io's wanderings from Argos till she reached the Delta.

37. Translate last two paragraphs of the Hypothesis.

38. Name the extant plays of Æschylus.

DEMOSTHENES DE CORONA.

1. Give dates of birth and death of Demosthenes, and place and circumstances of his death.

2. Who were his guardians, and how did they discharge their trust?

3. On what occasion did he first appear in court?

4. When did he first appear in public affairs?

5. What public offices did he fill?

6. What was the main purpose of his public career?

7. Date of indictment of Ctesiphon and of the Speech on the Crown.

8. What were the legal grounds of the indictment alleged by Æschines?

9. Why was the Speech of Æschines against Ctesiphon, and not against Demosthenes?

10. How did Demosthenes meet the legal charges?

11. What were the strong points of his defence?

12. How was the time allotted to the speakers determined?

13. Translate Cap. XIII.

14. Explain the terms γραφή, δίκη, ἀντωμοσια, διώκων, φεύγων, ἐλεῖν δίκην, προβούλευμα, ψήφισμα.

15. Translate Cap. XVIII. to ὀργιζόμενοι.

16. Give causes and results of Sacred War.

17. Explain ἂν ἰφησθῆναι.

18. Translate Cap. 29 to ποισυμένους.

19. What were the divisions and duties of the Archons?

20. How did the Athenians divide the year, and reckon the days of the month? Give the different expressions.

21. Explain the expression ἕνῃ παὶ νέᾳ.

22. What was the βουλή? how divided? and what is meant by φυλῆς πρυτανευοίσης Πανδιονίδος? give full explanation.

23. Give some account of the φυλαί and δῆμοι.

24. On what does δεδόχθαι depend?

25. What is said of the genuineness of the documents introduced in this speech, and for what reasons?

26. What were the modes of voting? and what is the proper meaning of χειροτονέω?

27. Translate Cap. 52.

28. What is the statement of Ulpian with regard to the pronunciation of μισθωτός, and the object of Demosthenes?

29. Ταμελιῶνος ἕκτῃ ἀπιόντος, what day of the month?

30. Translate the Decree of the Byzantines.

31. Give Doric forms and equivalents.

32. Explain the allusion to Attic usages in ἀλειτουργήτοις τᾶν λειτουργιᾶν.

III. GEOGRAPHY.

MODERN.

[The entrance examinations in Modern Geography are in general conducted orally, and are intended to cover not merely physical and political Geography, but also to test the student's general knowledge. The following questions were asked at the examination in June, 1882, and afford a good idea both as to the quality and quantity of what each candidate for admission is likely to be called upon to answer.]

1. What is the Gulf Stream? Describe fully, stating its effects.

2. What are latitude and longitude? Measured from what? What are lat. and long. of New York?

3. Name chief mountain ranges of the U. S., giving their general direction and situation. What great range in South America?

4. Name the great lakes N. of the U. S. Their outlet? Into what does it empty?

5. Principal rivers of the U. S.? Name states on the S. bank of Ohio R. On N. bank?

6. Bound France; Spain; Belgium. Principal rivers of Spain? What separates France from Germany?

7. Describe course of the Rhine.

8. Capital of Spain? Portugal? Norway? Sweden?

9. How many states compose the German Empire? Name the principal N. German states. The S. German? Who is at the head of the German government?

ANCIENT,

1881.

1. Bound Greece, Asia Minor, Arcadia, Bœotia, Phrygia, Cappadocia. Name principal mts., rivers, gulfs, and cities of Greece, beginning from the N.

2. What islands in Ægean Sea and what cities on W. coast of Asia Minor? Where was Susa? Ecbatana? Babylon? Alexandria? Cyrene? Carthage?

3. Name the ancient divisions of Gaul; of Spain.

4. Principal rivers of Gaul and their courses?

5. What was the Roman name of Marseilles, Lyons, Paris?

6. Chief cities of Spain?

7. Bound Latium. Why was Sicily called Trinacrium? Name capes of Sicily.

IV. ENGLISH.

[NOTE.—The entrance examinations are sometimes conducted orally and sometimes in writing. Students preparing are advised to give particular attention to pp. 67-71 of Quackenbos's Rhetoric.]

FRESHMAN EXAMINATION IN RHETORIC.

Criticise the following extracts.

Point out and define the figures that occur, stating which are faulty and why. Explain any violations of the essential properties of style. Name the elements of sublimity or beauty that you may find in any of the selections.

"Ye ice-falls! ye that from the mountain's brow
Adown enormous ravines slope amain—
Torrents, methinks, that heard a mighty voice,
And stopped at once amid their maddest plunge!
Motionless torrents! silent cataracts!
Who made you glorious as the gates of heaven
Beneath the keen full moon? Who bade the sun
Clothe you with rainbows? Who with living flowers
Of loveliest blue, spread garlands at your feet?
God! let the torrents, like a shout of nations,
Answer! and let the ice-plains echo, God!
And they, too, have a voice—yon piles of snow,
And in their perilous fall shall thunder, God!"
                                        —*Coleridge.*

Sensational papers are calculated to injure the morals.—I shall take them up one by one in anatomical order; that is to say, I shall proceed *a capite ad calcem.*—To Adam, Paradise was a home; to the good among his descendants, Home is a paradise.

"Thence up he flew, and on the tree of life
Sat like a cormorant."

I see before me the gladiator lie.—Flynn pursued the ancient avocation of picking pockets.—The date palm will not fruit without its roots are well watered.—Sweets to the sweet.—To out-herod Herod.—A cat in gloves catches no mice.—Language is the amber in which a thousand precious thoughts have been preserved.—I have noticed the word "party"· used for an individual occurring in Shakespeare.

"Traitors may talk of England's going down
In quicksands which their coward selves have sown—
She swims in hearts like these!"

Harrison Morrill had a very narrow escape from death recently. He was fastening the foreleg of an ox preparatory to shoeing, when he put his hind leg forward and over his neck, bringing his head and face in contact with the sling, tearing the flesh from one half of his forehead to the bone.—*N. E. Newspaper*.

> " But thousands die without or this or that ;
> Die, and endow a college or a cat."

A pious fraud.—High interest, bad security.—Loquacious age.— Raven tresses.—Hungry fire.—"Stonewall" Jackson.—Fond roof.— Winged words.—Shattered hopes.—And now, sir, I must embark into the feature on which this subject hinges.—Confusion on thy banners wait.—He is shaky on that doctrine.—Her almost childhood.—I heard this from the driver, who heard it from the postman, who was at the gate.—Why resurrect that old theory?—He said that that "that" that that man considered was not that "that" that he mentioned.—It may be of advantage to briefly recapitulate these facts.—The Tory party is satiated with, if not proud of, past gains.—The others shall have used every tittle of the same matter without planting one murmur in the heart.

Name the three great families of languages. To which of these does English belong? Give an account of the emigrations from the original home of the Aryans, the settlement of Britain, and the changes which took place in the language of that island until modern English was formed. For what elements is our tongue indebted to the Danish? to the Norman French? to the Celtic? to the Latin?

EXAMINATION FOR FRESHMAN SCHOLARSHIP IN RHETORIC.

Give Bain's definition of Rhetoric. What are the three principal ends in speaking, and to what three departments of the human mind do they correspond?

What is a figure of speech? What are the Figures of Similarity? Prove that the tracing of resemblances is natural to the human mind. Is Resemblance always a figure of speech?

What three places may the principal subject of the sentence occupy? Illustrate.

What does Bain say of Clearness? What of melody in words?

[NOTE.—As the department of English is to be entirely reorganized at the beginning of the college year 1882-3, no further papers in English are given here, as the course of study is expected to be completely altered.]

V. CHEMISTRY.

SOPHOMORE CLASS. INTERMEDIATE EXAM.

1. Define Matter. What forces does Matter possess? Kinds of Matter?

2. Define Polarity. How may Repulsion be demonstrated experimentally?
3. Atomic force?
4. Oxygen : its occurrence in nature, discovery, preparation, functions?—Ozone?
5. Hydrogen?
6. Kinds of Carbon? Functions and uses?
7. The Atmosphere? Composition?
8. Nitrogen?
9. Oxyhydrogen blow-pipe?
10. Structure of flame?

(FINAL EXAMINATION 1879.)

1. Bunsen burner? The Davy safety lamp?
2. Sources of impurities in water?
3. Iodine, Bromine, Fluorine, Chlorine.
4. Sulphur.
5. Symbols for Carbon, Sulphur, Water, Ozone, Ammonia, Marsh Gas, Coal Gas, Nitrous Oxide, Sulphuretted Hydrogen, Nitrous Oxide, Carbonic Acid, Chlorine, Sulphurous Acid?
6. Preparation of Coal Gas.
7. Give composition of principal mineral waters and describe fully.

EXAMINATION FOR SOPHOMORE SCHOLARSHIP IN CHEMISTRY.
1879.

1. Dalton's Atomic Theory and Law of Chemical Combination.
2. Quantivalence of the Elements.
3. Describe process of photography.
4. CO_2. Causes of impurities in air.
5. " Hard " water.
6. Preparation of Coal Gas.
7. Analysis of air.
8. Expansion and contraction of Water? Specific Gravity?
9. Latent Heat.
10. Spectrum Analysis.

VI. HISTORY.

[Candidates for admission are now examined in Ancient History (Greece, Rome, and Persia so far as it was brought into connection with Greece.) Rawlinson's Manual is recommended. As the first examinations under the new requirements were those of 1882, the papers were not obtained early enough for insertion in this work.

JUNIOR CLASS.
1880.

1. Give an account of the overthrow of Richard II., and explain the title of Henry IV. to the English throne.

2. What great events and discoveries mark the beginning of the sixteenth century, as the dividing point between mediæval and modern history? How did these things influence English History?

3. Explain the divorce question and the successive steps by which the English Reformation was carried through.

4. What dangers threatened Queen Elizabeth on her accession, and by what policy did she attempt to meet them?

5. What was the policy of the successive Tudor sovereigns toward Parliament?

6. What were the claims of Parliament over against the Stuart sovereigns as shown in the Petition of Rights, 1628; by the acts of the Long Parliament, 1640; and the Bill of Rights, 1689?

7. What seems to have been Oliver Cromwell's idea of government in England, and how did he actually rule?

8. Did the Puritan Rebellion of 1642–1660 accomplish anything, and if so, what?

9. When and by what title did the House of Hanover come to the English throne?

10. What was the dominant influence in the government of England during the 18th century, and what circumstances determined this?

SENIOR CLASS, 1881.

(Constitutional History of the U. S.)

1. What is meant by the principle of Ultimate Sovereignty?

2. Describe the different forms of Colonial Government.

3. Where was the ultimate sovereignty under the Confederation?

4. What guarantee does the Constitution contain for *personal* protection?

5. What were the Virginia and Kentucky Resolutions?

6. What was the first violation of the Constitution of 1789?

7. What was the Missouri Compromise?

8. Give Webster's and also Calhoun's theory of the Constitution.

VII. POLITICAL ECONOMY.

JUNIOR CLASS, 1880.

1. Give a history of the English Poor Laws.

2. What do you mean by Co-operation? What are the supposed advantages to the laborer? Explain the system of the Rochdale Equitable Pioneers and of the Schultze-Delitsch Credit-Banks.

3. What determines the rate of wages of labor, and what effect does the customary food of laborers have on their wages?

4. Explain the following sentence: "It will be clear that the machinery of a Trade's Union cannot increase wages by depressing the profits of capital."

5. Explain and illustrate the following : "Banks of issue find it possible to circulate a far larger amount of paper than the gold on which the paper is based." What effect does the abstraction of gold have in such a case ?

6. What is meant by an income tax ; on what part of the income should it be levied and why ?

. 7. Explain the origin of the Irish cottier system of land tenure, its evils and the proposed remedy.

8. Explain the following sentences from the text book :

"It (Protection) inflicts actual suffering or inconvenience on the public in order to secure a *delusive* benefit to individuals." "It will be clear also that the Protection cannot stimulate general industry." "In fact, whenever it (the state) protects particular kinds of labor it diminishes capital." "Every country enjoys a natural protection to its manufactures."

VIII. PSYCHOLOGY.

JUNIOR CLASS.

1. In following lines point out the influence of the Association of Ideas on the Imagination :

(a).
> " How wonderful is Death !
> Death and his brother, Sleep.
> One pale as yonder wan and horned moon,
> With lips of lurid blue;
> The other glowing like the vital moon
> When throned on Ocean's waves
> It breathes over the world;
> Yet both so passing strange and wonderful !"
> —*Shelley*.

(b).
> " Be near me when my life is low
> When the blood creeps and the nerves prick
> And tingle, and the heart is sick
> And all the wheels of Being slow.
>
> *   *   *   *   *   *   *   *
>
> Be near me when my faith is dry,
> And men the flies of latter spring
> That lay their eggs and sting and sing,
> And weave their petty cells and die."
> —*Tennyson*.

2. What is the difference between Perception and Conception ?

3. Show that the ideas of Cause and Effect can not be empirically derived.

4. Can there be an emotion without knowledge to excite emotion ?

5. Is self free to will ?

6. Is man responsible ?

IX. LOGIC.

JUNIOR CLASS, 1880.

A. I. Define Logic. What characteristics have the Laws of Thought ?

II. What is a *singular* term, a *concrete* term, a *general* term, a *collective* term, an *abstract* term ?

III. Which of the following terms are concrete ? *City, Grandeur, Black, Who, Friendship.* Which of the following are abstract ? *Childhood, Book, Reason.*

IV. What is the *quantity* and *quality* of the following propositions ?

Few men become great.

Most great men are vain.

Thousands were not unmoved by the sight.

Not a few of the Greeks were philosophers.

B. I. Define *Middle Term, Major Premise, Enthymeme, Sorites, Mood, Figure, Illicit Process, Fallacy of Composition, Fallacy of Accident.*

II. What figure must have a negative conclusion ? Why ?

III. If one premise be O what must the other be ? Why ?

IV. Why is O A O invalid in the fourth figure ?

V. To what fallacy does A A A in the second figure give rise ?

SYLLOGISMS.

1. No man can serve two masters; therefore I may serve three masters.

2. It is a mistake to suppose that infidelity causes immorality ; for many infidels lead moral lives while many believers act immorally.

3. My client is a very worthy man; his accuser is a man of bad character, therefore it is unlikely that my client should have done that of which he has been accused.

4. If this man has a good political record, he should be re-elected. If he befriended the poor he should be re-elected. If he is a man of wealth he should be re-elected. Now, although he has no money and so has not befriended the poor, he has a good political record. Therefore he should be re-elected.

X. HISTORY OF PHILOSOPHY.

Senior Class, Intermediate Examination : 1881.

1. What was the first systematic development of Greek thought ?
2. Give account of the theory of Parmenides the Eleatic.
3. Give account of doctrines of Heracleitus.
4. What were the chief sources of Plato's Dialectic ?
5. What did Aristotle mean by Ethical Virtue ?
6. Compare the Ethics of the Stoics with that of the Epicureans.
7. Into what two periods may the Patristic Age be divided, and against whom were the polemics of the later fathers directed ?
8. Give brief account of Abelard's philosophy.
9. Give the Christian Aristotelians and show how they combined theology with philosophy.

Final Examination : 1881.

1. Name and define the Idols of the Baconian philosophy.
2. What is the defect of Bacon's method ?
3. According to Hobbes, how does the Commonwealth arise from man's natural state ?
4. In what way did Locke explain the origin of our ideas ?
5. Explain the following terms of Locke's Philosophy : *Simple and Complex Ideas ; Modes ; Substances.*
6. What was the foundation of Berkeley's Idealism ?
7. What is Berkeley's doctrine as to the general notion or idea ?
8. How did Hume reach the position of maintaining that all knowledge is of impressions and ideas ?
9. Show the difference between Hume's belief and Berkeley's ideas as to Mind ?
10. How did Reid oppose Hume and on what foundation did he endeavor to raise a constructive system ?
11. Explain Thomas Brown's doctrine of perception.
12. What is meant by the Relativity Theory of knowledge ?
13. What is John Stuart Mill's doctrine of Cause and Effect ?

XI. GEOLOGY.

Senior Class Intermediate Exam., 1881.

1. Give the Nebular Hypothesis.
2. Give the four groups of minerals of the common rocks.
3. Kinds of rocks ?   The Gulf Stream ?

4. Three conditions of rock masses, with positions of strata?

5. Divisions of Geological Time?

6. Rocks of the Archæan era—kinds and distribution?

7. The Lower Silurian?

8. Periods of the Upper Silurian era, with rocks of each?

FINAL EXAMINATION, 1881.

1. Give an account of the Devonian Age.

2. Give an account of the flora and fauna of the Carboniferous Age.

3. Explain the formation of coal beds, with an account of some of them.

4. Divisions of the Reptilian age, and named from what?

5. Flora and fauna of the first two periods?

6. How are the Tertiary strata divided?

7. Periods of the Quaternary Age? Give some account of each.

XII. LATIN.

ENTRANCE EXAMINATION.

1. Translate Cæsar, B. G., I. from *Gallis magno* to *cœperunt*, and VI., 20.

2. Decline *scutis, pedem, manu, rumore,* and *vulneribus,* adding of what Declension and Gender each is, and the characteristic of the Declension.

3. Decline *nudo, uno,* and *pluribus,* describing the classes of adjective according to Declension.

4. Compare *multi, summis, falsis,* and *prima,* giving chief rules of Comparison.

5. Decline *quæ, se, alio,* and *quis,* and define each class of pronouns.

6. Give principal parts of all verbs in second passage; state of what conjugation each verb in first passage is, and when the form is made.

7. Translate Cic. in Cat. II., ix., from *Hi dum ædificant.* Translate Cic. pro Lege Manil. xxii., 65 and 66.

8. Give rules of syntax for Case or Agreement, or both, of all nouns, adjectives and pronouns in first three lines of first passage, and for use of all infinitive and subjunctives in second passage.

9. Translate Æneid, III. 294–305, and VI. 548–556.

10. Describe metre of the above, and mark off feet and metrical pause of first five verses.

11. Give rule of Quantity for each syllable in first three verses.

12. Translate into Latin: (*a*) You seized that town on the first of

November. (*b*) I found out this when your meeting had broken up. (*c*) The eyes of many will watch you. (*d*) I think your house ought to be left by you. (*e*) A little while ago you could distinctly hear their voices. (*f*) You understand what he thinks of you. (*g*) No one is so bad as not to admit this. (*h*) Two knights were found to free .you from that trouble.

FRESHMAN CLASS. ODES OF HORACE.

1. Give the principal events of the life of Horace, with the dates of his birth and death.

2. Name his works in the probable order of their publication.

3. What peculiar character distinguishes the ode from other kinds of poetry? Was this distinction at first peculiar to any one species of poetical composition?

4. Under what four denominations may all odes be comprised?

5. In what points may Horace be said to excel as regards the style of his composition in the odes?

6. What class of Greek poets did he especially imitate? Name three of this class.

7. What was the *Carmen Seculare?* What the subject of the epistle to the Pisones?

8. To whom do we probably owe the term Epode, and to what peculiarity of the poem, so-called, has the word particular reference?

9. Translate, scan and prove Ode I., 16, 13–16.

10. What is the Complementary Infinitive? Quote examples from the odes. In all cases of its occurrence with an adjective what broad resemblance holds?

11. What two constructions with verbs of changing and exchanging? Which the more common? Give an example of each?

12. Translate I., 11.

13. Substitute two forms of the Imperative for *ne quaesieris*.

14 The construction of *scire nefas* and of *quem—dederint?*

15. Analyze *ut melius quidquid erit pati*.

16. *Sapias, Liques.* When may the second person of the Present Subjunctive be substituted for the Imperative in prose? When in poetry?

17. Translate I., 17, 24–28.

18. What construction follows verbs of fearing?

19. Compare the force of *male* here with that of the same word in I., 9, 24.

20. Translate I., 18, 7–16.

21. *Plus nimio.* Account in two ways for the ablative.

22. *Arcanique fides prodiga.* What figure of rhetoric here? Derive and define it.

23. Translate I., 31, 17–20.

24. *Frui paratis valido mihi dones.* Change the form and construction of these words to suit prose.

25. Quote Juvenal in illustration of the thought expressed in this stanza.

26. Translate I., 34.

27. What two principal systems of philosophy current at Rome in Horace's time? Of what state of mind with reference to each of these would this ode seem to be an expression? What and where expressed in his writings is the doctrine that is here apparently surrendered?

28. Give a rule for the use of the genitive after *consultus.*

29. Why place a comma after *plerumque* rather than after *dividens?*

30. Derive and explain *Diespiter, bruma, sobrius, tragœdia, fastus.*

31. Translate II., 3, 21–28.

32. Analyze the construction in *Divesne—moreris.* What the case of *victima*, and why?

33. What feet compose the Sapphic verse? Quote an example. Where in the line does the principal caesura fall?

34. Translate into Latin:—

Thou shalt not kill. The keepers are to guard the gates; they are not to sleep. The general shut the gates of the camp that the enemy might not rush into the camp with the fleeing recruits. If you had called the physician, you would have been delivered from the disease. If you were industrious you would be praised. Would that we had preserved our liberty. Would that the man were setting up the statue in our garden. May the enemy not carry the city. O Gajus Julius Cæsar, thou hast saved the state, but thou hast destroyed freedom.

CICERO DE SENECTUTE.

1. What is the peculiar form in which both the Cato Major and the Laelius are cast?

2. What reason for adopting this form as given in opening chapter of the Laelius?

3. Supposed date of Cato's discourse? Scene of the Laelius laid in midst of what revolution?

4. Give family tree, with names in full, of Scipios mentioned in Cato Major.

5. Who are *dramatis personæ* in the Laelius? The friendship of what two men forms ground of discussion?

6. Translate *De Senec.* XI. to *cogimur.*

7. *Ne sint ;* account for mode. On what may the clause be said to depend ?

8. *Non modo ;* what word omitted after *modo?* Under what conditions does this omission generally occur?

9. Translate XV. from *quid ego* to *delectent.*

10. Account for mode in *commemorem, noscatis, procreet, delectent.*

11. Derive *ortus, satus, incrementa,* from their verbs.

12. Derive and define *malleoli, sarmenta, viviradices, propagines.*

13. Translate XXIII. from *quod quidem* to *non videre.*

14. Account for five subjunctives in the passage.

15. What is dependence of *ut—essent?*

16. In phrase *quid quod* what is omitted? Hence what the dependence of *quod—moritur?*

17. Supply what is omitted between *ille* and *vivere.*

18. Translate XXII., from *sic mihi* to *rocordari.*

19, Turn words from *quum* to *relicturus* into *oratio recta.*

20. What is meant by *principium motus?*

21. What distinction between *interire* and *perire?*

22. Analyze construction from *magno* to *recordari,* and account for subjunctives.

23. From what writings of what author are these ideas on the immortality of the soul chiefly borrowed?

24. What customs denoted by following infinitives : *Salutari, appeti, decedi, assurgi, deduci, reduci, consuli?*

25. Translate into Latin : Would that the Master were setting up the statue in our garden.—The herdsman killed the wolves lest they should devour the lambs.—The keepers are to guard the gates ; they are not to sleep.—The Romans conquered their enemies both on sea and land.

FRESHMAN SCHOLARSHIP IN LATIN.

1. Translate Cic. De Senec. XXII., from *atque etiam* to *servabitis.*

2. Form the above into *oratio obliqua,* depending on a verb of past time.

3. Derive and define: *deliratio, quincunx, elogium, devorsorium, compagibus, imperium, synephebis, consitiones, insitiones, vineis, arbustis, examinibus.*

4. What four causes of complaint against old age are successively discussed by Cato ?

5. What is shown by use of subjunctive in statement of these causes.

6. Translate into Ciceronian Latin : I have no reason for finding fault with old age. To the old age of Appius Claudius it was added also,

that he was blind. According to our practice, fathers who manage their affairs badly are wont to be interdicted from their possessions. I could wish, to be sure, that I were able to make the same boast as Cyrus. O, wretched old man, not to have seen in so long a life, that death should be despised, which either is wholly to be regarded with indifference if it entirely annihilates the soul, or even is to be wished for, if it leads to some place where it is going to be eternal. But the old man has not even anything to hope for. For we must surely die and perhaps this very day.*

Sophomore Class.

Satires of Horace.

1. Write a brief life of Horace, describing his works and giving date of the production of each.

2. Translate I Sat. VI. 110–131.

3. *Hoc:* what form does Horace interchange with this? *Milibus atque aliis:* remark fully a position of *atque* here and state whether this position occurs in Virgil. *Quacunque libido est—quanti olus ac far:* supply ellipsis in each case here, and remark on the second. *Vespertinum:* what is the force of this, what could you substitute for it, and what other instance of the same usage have you had? *Lapis albus:* how otherwise was this distinguished? *Echinus:* what other two words have you had for this? *Campana supellex:* what does this mean and what term was used in contrast with it? *Obeundus Marsya qui etc.:* explain this allusion fully. *Unguor olivo Non quo,* etc.: show that there was no exaggeration here. *Suavius ac si:* what is the meaning of *ac* here, and how did it acquire this meaning?

4. Translate, I Sat. X. 1–19.

5. What can you say to relieve the abruptness of the beginning of this satire? *Lucili:* give some account of this writer, and state when Horace has mentioned him before. *Sale:* what two figurative ideas are implied in this word here? *Pulchra poemata:* give an equivalent for this. *Nec hoc tribuens dederim altera:* what kind of a sentence is this, and what would be the common form? *Lassas onerantibus:* give various instances of this juxtaposition of words and explain each. *Vicem:* what word can be substituted for this? *Secat:* explain the figure here. *Comoedia prisca:* describe different classes of Gk. Comedy. *Simius iste:* who is probably meant by this? *Calvum, Catullum:* give an account of these two authors and the other names of the group to which the latter belonged.

6. Give rule of quantity for the italicised vowels in the following

---

*In scholarship examinations the special examination usually has a weight of about ⅓; the general exam., ⅔.

words : fecerat, unguibus, divellere, mordicus, caput, fortuna, secundus, pedem, turgidus, ego.

7. Give derivation, or composition, or both, of the following, adding any illustration or explanation that you can : nempe, dico (*to say*), versus, magnus, fero, tam, ignosco, pullus (*dark colored*) lex, scalpo.

GERMANIA AND AGRICOLA OF TACITUS.

1. State what is known of the life of Tacitus, adding names of the great authors belonging to the same period with him.

2. Give some account of his various writings, stating the probable reason why his principal works have come down to us in imperfect condition, and of which work the authenticity has been questioned and on what grounds.

3. Mention some of the characteristics of his style, adding illustrations, and state whom of the Romans he seems to have imitated, and whom of the Greeks.

4. Translate Germania, XVI.

5. *populis :* how do you decide whether this is a dative or an ablative ? *satis notum est :* remark on this use of *satis* and give another instance of it from Tacitus.

ac : what is the general distinction between the use of *atque* and *ac* ? *ut fons, ut campus, etc. :* remark on the repetition of the particle here. *in nostrum morem :* how else does Tacitus say this ? *suam quisque domum :* quote the case in which Tacitus departs from this order. *remedium :* what two distinct meanings had this word ? *citra speciem aut delectationem :* why does *aut*, not *ac* stand here, as below *picturam ac lineamenta ? suffugium hiemi et receptaculum frugibus:* how does Tacitus vary this construction ? *rigorum frigorum :* are these words etymologically connected ?

6. Translate German : XLV. to *Germanorum inertia laborant.*

7. *Suionas :* account for this Greek form, and give the names kindred to this.

mare pigrum : what was the cause of this, and how does Tacitus elsewhere explain it ? *cingi cludique :* what is the construction of these infinitives ? *cludi :* in what part of this verb does he use another form and of what other word does he use a bye-form ? *sonum-adicit :* explain these phenomena, give Halm's reading for *deorum*, and account for the number of *capitis. Suevici maris :* what is the modern name of this, and the ancient designation of the Southern part ? *Germanorum inertia :* explain this, and give other characteristics of the Germani and allied races, mentioned by Tacitus.

8. Translate Agric. IX., to *sordidum arbitrabatur.*

JUNIOR CLASS.
Satires of Juvenal.

1. What is known of the life of Juvenal?

2. State the argument of the satire—*semper ego auditor tantum? Numquamne reponam.*

3. Translate I. Sat. I. 127-146.

4. *Spatula:* what changes in meaning did this word undergo? *jurisque peritus Apollo:* explain allusion. *Nescio quis:* what is the usual force of this expression, and what pronoun does Juvenal use as an equivalent to it? *Arabarchus:* what other reading here, and what explanation of each? *ignis:* what word would regularly have stood here, and what other word does Juvenal jocosely use to designate a poor man's fuel? *orbibus:* what two words are synonymous with this and what term have you had in Horace for the table of the poor? *Luxuriæ sordes:* what is common form of this expression and what advantage has this form? *convivia:* what is the meaning of the word here and what does Cic. say of its full and proper force?

5. What is the subject of the Satire—*Ecce iterum Crispinus?*

6. Translate I. Sat. IV. 136-154.

7. *Falerno:* describe place where this wine and the Calenum were produced. *Tempestate:* distinguish *tempus, tempestas* and *procella, Circeis Lucrinum Saxum, Rutupino fundo:* describe these places. *Echinus:* what two things does this term signify in Nat. History? *Albanam arcem:* what place is meant by this and why is this word *arcem* used here? *diversis partibus orbis:* what word is *diversis* used for here and who had used this phrase before Juvenal? *cerdonibus Lamiarum:* derive *cerdonibus* and state what is the relation of these terms.

8. What is treated of in the Satire—*Si te propositi nondum pudet, etc?*

9. Translate I. Sat. V. 51-66.

10. *aliam:* here equivalent to *diversam:* give the proper distinction between the two words. *nigri Mauri:* account for the repetition of idea here, and give other instances of it. *Latinæ* and *calidæ gelidæque:* Supply ellipses here and add other cases of them. *Ne te teneam:* what is this use of subjunctive called, by what word is it properly translated, and what other phrases equivalent to this can you adduce from Juvenal and Horace? *sed forma, sed aetas:* state what is peculiar in this rare use of the adversative conjunction and cite other instances of it.

(1881). Translate into Dactylic Hexameters:—
"Aurora brought fair light to wretched men,
Renewing all their work and all their toil."

Translate into Elegiacs:—
"And so through all your life your hearts were one,
Firm to the end your faithful trust."

CICERO DE OFFICIIS.

1. Give a brief sketch of Roman Philosophy, describing the chief works that have come down to us.

2. What natural causes made the Romans inferior to the Greeks in this study?

3. State what gave occasion to this treatise, from what sources Cicero informs us that it was drawn, adding the Argument of the First Book.

4. Translate I. v., 14, 15.

5. *honestum:* what is meant by this term here, and how does it differ from the term now employed by philosophy for this purpose?

6. *quattuor partium:* what are the simple designations of the qualities here described?

7. *in—versatur:* give the various equivalents which Cicero employs for this.

8. *in quo inest:* what other construction, common in later Latin, might stand here?

9. *ex ea parte—inest:* account for the occurrence of this solecism.

10. *Ut—solet:* point out the irregularity of form in this period.

11. *rite:* what is the collateral form of this, and what analogous cases can you adduce?

12. Translate I. xi., 35 and 36.

13. *ob eam causam, ut:* what might you substitute for the antecedent in this formula?

14. *immanes:* give the ancient and the modern derivation of this word.

15. *Tusculanos—Hernicos:* which people of these five was first admitted to the *Civitas Romana,* and at what date?

16. *Karthaginem—Numantiam—Corinthum:* what are the dates of the events here alluded to, and what was the avowed reason for the reduction of Corinth?

17. *quae—habitura sit—quos vi deviceris:* why have these clauses the subjunctive mood, and how may you change the form of the first without changing the sense?

18. *si non—at:* what particle is sometimes found with *at* in this formula?

19. *earum patroni essent:* give instances of this from Roman History.

20. Translate I. xxvii., 94.

21. *nec vero agere quidquam:* supply the ellipsis here, and cite other cases of remarkable ellipsis in this work.

22. *causam probabilem :* from what does Cicero distinguish this in the introduction to this work ?

23. *appetitus rationi :* what does Cicero say elsewhere of these, what is the modern division of the powers of the mind, and by what circumlocutions does Cicero denote the Sensibility?

24. *constantia :* in what different senses does Cicero employ this term ?

25. *animi—corpora :* remark on the use of the plural here, and in abstract nouns, as *fortitudines*, and the like.

JUNIOR SCHOLARSHIP IN LATIN : 1880.

Cicero De Officiis.

1. Translate : $\begin{cases} \text{I., x., 33, from } \textit{existunt} \text{ to } \textit{proverbium.} \\ \text{I., xii., 37.} \\ \text{I., iv., 11.} \end{cases}$

2. *Sed malitosa* : what difficulty lies in these words and if, against some authorities, they are retained, how can we meet the difficulty ?

3. *Vocaretur :* what is the force of the Subjunctive and what troublesome irregularity is there in the form of the sentence ?

4. In comparing man with the lower animals, what points of difference and what of agreement does Cicero indicate?

5. *Non male :* what adverbs, by the usage of Cicero elsewhere, might take the place of this negative expression ?

6. *Operam exigendam esse :* state what is the construction of the infinitive here and give other instances of it. *Uti ut :* if Cicero had cared to avoid the use of *ut* after *uti* what adverbs had he the choice of?

7. What is the difference between the use of *etiam* in the first and second sentences, and what third and uncommon use of it have you had ?

SENIOR CLASS.

QUINTILIAN, TENTH BOOK.*

1. Give the principal facts in the life of Quintilian.

2. What evidence is there that he received his early education in Rome?

3. State briefly the contents of the several books of the Institutes.

4. Give some account of Cicero's great work on the same subject, adding a comparison of the two.

5. What are Cicero's other works on the same subject?

6. Translate

In lectione certius iudicium, quod audienti frequenter aut suus cuique favor aut ille laudantium clamor extorquet. Pudet enim dissen-

---

* Examinations of the Senior Class have of late been partly oral. The paper given above was used in 1872.

tire, et velut tacita quadam verecundia inhibemur plus nobis credere, cum interim et vitiosa, pluribus placent, et a corrogatis laudantur etiam quae non placent. Sed e contrario quoque accidit, ut optime dictis gratiam prava iudicia non referant. Lectio libera est nec actionis impetu transcurrit ; sed repetere saepius licet, sive dubites sive memoriae affigere velis. Repetamus autem et tractemus, et ut cibos mansos ac prope liquefactos demittimus, quo facilius digerantur, ita lectio non cruda, sed multa iteratione mollita et velut confecta, memoriae imitationique tradatur.

7. *interim :* what particle would have stood here in the earlier Latin ?

8. *a corrogatis laudantur :* how does Pliny the Younger designate these persons ?

9. *e contrario :* what is the more usual form for this ?

10. *optime dictis :* explain and illustrate the presence here of an adverb with a word commonly used as a noun.

11. *Repetamus—et tractemus :* if the view be adopted that the prefix *re-* affects both verbs in this passage, what illustration of it can be adduced ?

12. *quo facilius digerantur :* state under what circumstances *ut* and *quo* interchanged as final particles, and what was the probable origin of the use of *quo* in such a clause as this.

13. Translate.

Plurimum dicit oratori conferre Theophrastus lectionem poetarum, multique eius iudicium sequuntur; neque immerito. Namque ab his in rebus spiritus et in verbis sublimitas et in affectibus motus omnis et in personis decor petitur, praecipueque velut attrita cotidiano actu forensi ingenia optime rerum talium blanditia reparantur. Ideoque in hac lectione Cicero requiescendum putat. Meminerimus tamen non per omnia poetas esse oratori sequendos, nec libertate verborum nec licentia figurarum ; genus ostentationi comparatum, et praeter id, quod solam petit voluptatem eamque etiam fingendo non falsa modo, sed etiam quaedam incredibilia secatur, patrocinio quoque aliquo iuvari : quod alligata ad certam pedum necessitatem non semper uti propriis possit, sed depulsa recta via necessario ad eloquendi quaedam deverticula confugiat, nec mutare quaedam modo verba, sed extendere, corripere, convertere, dividere cogatur; nos vero armatos stare in acie et summis de rebus decernere et ad victoriam niti. Neque ero arma squalere situ ac rubigine velim, sed fulgorem inesse qui terreat, qualis est ferri, quo mens simul visusque praestringitur non qualis auri argentique, imbellis et potius habenti periculosus.

14. *neque immerito. Namque :* what are the other forms of this formula, and what is the Greek equivalent ?

15. *Cicero—putat :* what is referred to here ?

16. *mutare—extendere, corripere, convertere, dividere cogatur :*

give in Latin one or more instances of each kind of poetic license alluded to in these words.

17. *auri argentique:* is this the invariable order of these ideas in Latin ?

THE ANDRIAN OF TERENCE.

1. What are the leading facts in the life of Terence?

2. Mention his Plays in the order of performance, and state why it is supposed that we have all the Plays he wrote.

3. Give briefly the Plot of the Andrian, and state what imitations there are of it in the French and in the English Drama.

4. Translate Act I., iv. 46–73.

5. *Quas credis esse has :* State what pronoun *Quas* stands for here, explain the attraction of *has*, and quote other similar cases of attraction in this Play.

6. *Quor :* What is the origin of this word, and under what other forms does it occur ?

7. *gnati :* Account for the presence of the guttural here and illustrate it.

8. *excessit ex ephebis* and *nequid nimis :* Give the Greek original for these expressions and add any other translations or imitations from the Greek in this Play.

9. *plerique omnes :* What writer before, and what one after, Terence, used this expression ?

10. *ad philosophos :* Supply the Ellipsis here, and add some of the frequent Ellipses that occur in Terence's style, illustrating them by English usage where you can.

11. *egregie praeter cetera :* Give other instances of repetition of ideas in Terence, colloquial or comical. .

12. *quibus erat quomque :* What figure of Syntax does this order fall under, and what other case of it occurs in what you have read?

13. *Obsequium amicos, veritas odium parit :* Give such other proverbs as you remember from Terence, and state what ancient writers quoted this.

14. *huc viciniae :* Give other special instances of this construction in this Play.

15. Translate Act II., Sc. II.–III., vv. 380–403.

16. *dictum ac factum :* What particle is this phrase equivalent to, and what illustrations can you give of the phrase ?

17. *eiciat :* Show how this form arose.

18. *Cedo :* Give the probable origin of this and of the plural form.

19. *Numquam faciam :* What verb does *faciam* represent here, what is the usage of Terence about the repetition of the verb in such case, and what illustrations of it from other languages can you give ?

www.ingramcontent.com/pod-product-compliance
Lightning Source LLC
Chambersburg PA
CBHW020244090426
42735CB00010B/1833